THE
Archive Photographs
SERIES

TORPOINT

HIGH TIDE in the late 1920s. A view from Gravesend taken by local photographer Alfred Collings.

THE
Archive Photographs
SERIES

TORPOINT

Compiled by
Pat and Freda Manning

CHALFORD

The Chalford Publishing Company
St Mary's Mill, Chalford,
Stroud, Gloucestershire, GL6 8NX

ISBN 0 7524 1002 4

Typesetting and origination by
The Chalford Publishing Company
Printed in Great Britain by
Bailey Print, Dursley, Gloucestershire

THE FERRY,1834-1871.

Contents

Acknowledgements

We should like to express our thanks to all the people of Torpoint who, over the years, have given us, or allowed us to copy, photographs. They have all been incorporated into the Torpoint Archives and it is from that collection that this book has been compiled. We have also drawn on the vast fund of knowledge we have acquired from the people of the town.

Pat and Freda Manning.
June 1997.

Carbeille School Friends' Association boat trip, 1973

Introduction

My wife and I came to Torpoint as young teachers over forty years ago. Probably due to the nature of our jobs and because we lived in the town our interest in its history grew. Inevitably we came into contact with the late Jack Kingston who, as a Torpointer born and bred, had developed an obsessional interest in the early history of Torpoint. This interest started as a boy, waned when he joined the Navy during the war, but resumed upon 'demob' in 1945. It is fair to say that Jack's study was from the beginnings of Torpoint to the end of the Second World War. Ours tended to be the social history of the 30s and 40s and what was going on around us. This worked out well because we pooled our knowledge and resources and ended up in the 70s with over four thousand photographs and records, cuttings and artefacts as well as a mass of what many regarded as 'old rubbish' but which has grown more valuable as time goes on. Unfortunately Jack Kingston died in 1984; his collection became our responsibility. The Torpoint Town Council, in 1983, gave support for the establishment of a 'home' for the collection in the Council Offices. The Torpoint Archives was formed with a band of 'friends'. With the help of our volunteer staff and the generosity of the townsfolk who have given or allowed us to copy photographs we now have a collection of over twelve thousand photographs. We also have a large collection of past records of the town, replacing much that was lost in the blitz in 1941. It is from this Archive that the photographs have been taken.

Pat Manning.
June 1997.

A 'GENUINE' CORNISH PASTY! Another photograph by taken A.J. Collings who recorded the town and its people from 1910 to 1940.

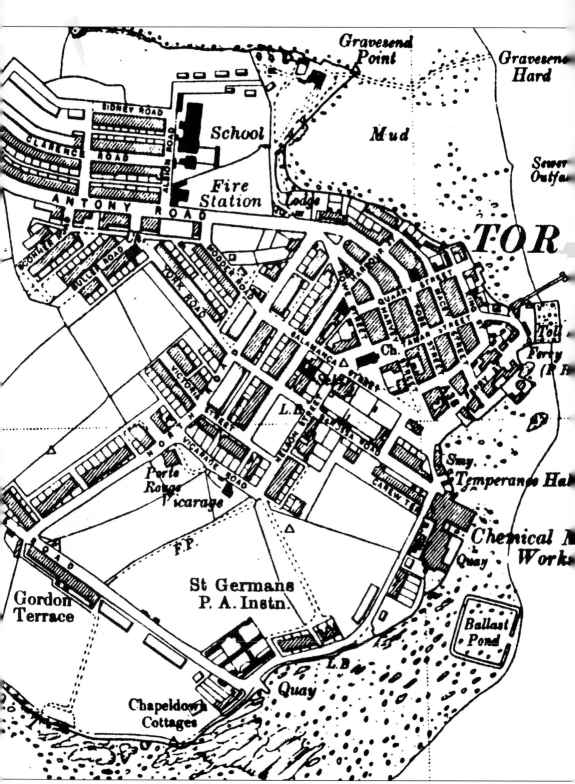

A map of Torpoint's town centre.

One
The Ferry

The single thing that has made Torpoint famous or, in some cases, infamous throughout the world has been its ferry. Without the chains under the River Tamar linking Cornwall to the Devon shore the county would have drifted away from England and probably have become part of some Mediterranean or African country, or so most of us in Torpoint firmly believe. However, over the years, it has been an efficient means of crossing the river. A bridge would have been quicker but the demands of the Admiralty for uninterrupted access to the harbour made the ferry a safer bet. In the light of the 1941 Blitz this was a justifiable decision. Traffic has increased considerably since the 1930s and constant upgrading has been needed. The ferry came into being in 1791 and the steam ferries were introduced in 1834. It is strange that the actual crossing time has remained about the same since those days.

STEAM FERRY. A group of gentlemen met and decided to take shares in the building and operating of a steam ferry across the River Tamar at Torpoint in November 1826. Unfortunately there are no photographs of the first steam ferry, the *Jemima*, but the photograph does show the first chain ferry designed by Rendell.

THE FIRST CHAIN FERRY. After the failure of the *Jemima* the proprietors looked for a reliable ferry to acquire. They approached Mr James Rendell who had designed a successful ferry at Dartmouth. His Torpoint ferry was opened to the public in 1834. The landing places on either side of the river were simple planes, sloping from two feet below low water mark to two feet above high water. The time taken to cross was eight minutes at high tide and seven minutes at low tide. This gave an average time on passage of seven and a half minutes, the same as in the 1990s. Men-of-War overshadow the ferry here and Keyham Steam Yard is in the background.

THE SECOND CHAIN FERRY, 1836-1878. A second ferry was acquired in 1836 and it ran on its own set of chains. It had a platform or carriage deck on either side with the engine compartment in the middle. It was fifty-five feet long and forty-five feet wide. It could carry three four-horse carriages, one pair-horse carriage, seven saddle horses and sixty foot passengers at one time. The foot passengers travelled on cross decks at either end of the engine compartment.

THE MAIL COACH. Once the turnpike road was built westwards from Torpoint, the mail coaches travelled on the ferries. In this print the *Quicksilver* is shown driving on to the ferry at Torpoint. The *Royal Quicksilver Mail* was owned by William Chaplin and ran from London to Falmouth. It was built for speed rather than passenger accommodation. It was painted red and black with small doors and scarlet wheels. It was the fastest mail coach and travelled at a speed of $10\frac{1}{2}$ miles an hour.

A THIRD FERRY. In 1871 the first of the original chain ferries was replaced by a new and larger one. It was very similar in design to the previous ones but had passenger seating above the engine compartment.

TRAVEL IN THE 1870s. A close-up of the ramps and foot passenger areas on the ferry. This ferry ran until 1925.

STEAMER ARRIVING AT THE PONTOON, TORPOINT.

THE TORPOINT LANDING STAGE. When the chain ferry stopped running at 9 p.m., a steamboat service took over. This enterprise began in 1895 and was run by Mr William Reynolds. The steamers ran from the pier, north of the ferry beach, to Pottery Quay, Devonport from 9 p.m. to midnight. The vessels were The *Dainty* and The *Link*.

THE LADY BEATRICE. The Reynolds' steamers ceased to cross the river in 1901 because increased landing fees made the service unprofitable. However, local feeling was such that a meeting between the parish council and the ferry proprietors resulted in the purchase of the steamer *Volta* to restart the service. She had a deck capacity of sixty passengers. In 1904 the *Lady Beatrice*, built at Waterman's Yard, Cremyll, joined the *Volta*. The steamer service ran until 1932 when the ferries began to run on a 24 hour basis.

A FOURTH FERRY. The second of the original chain ferries was replaced by another new one in 1878. It was larger and the first to have two funnels. It must have been a pioneer of prefabrication as the parts were made in workshops in Plymouth and assembled at the water's edge in Stonehouse. The ferry was controlled by a voice pipe with the driver looking out of a porthole. The prow was raised by a hand wheel amidships. It remained in service until 1926.

SIDE BY SIDE. The third ferry (on the right) and the fourth did not run at the same time. The smaller, single-funnelled ferry ran in the winter and the larger one in the summer. A flag was hoisted to show the direction in which it was travelling.

DEVONPORT LANDING STAGE. Horse-drawn wagons were the chief means of transporting goods from Plymouth to Torpoint. Advertising on the ferry is nothing new. 'Hocking Pianos and Organs' was a very familiar feature of the waterside when the ferry landed.

FERRY AT TORPOINT. The low tide enables the ferry chains to be seen very clearly. First to disembark from this crossing was the horseman who was probably an army officer stationed at Tregantle, Scraesdon or one of the other forts in the area.

THE WORCESTERSHIRE REGIMENT, which was a Special Reserve unit, was based at Fort Tregantle from August 1914 until the end of 1917. The CQMS in the foreground could be a Worcestershire man although his badge is not clear. The rest all appear to be wearing dark blue uniforms with white belts. The blue uniforms could be explained by a shortage of khaki. The men at the front on the right are bandsmen with 'wings' on their shoulders.

CROWDS GREETING A NEW FERRY, 1925. This new ferry, built by Messrs Phillips and Son, of Dartmouth, replaced the 1871 ferry. Old and young turned out to see the new ferry approach Torpoint.

NEW OWNERS. In 1920, the Cornwall County Council had acquired the ferry undertaking. Unfortunately for local people, the new owners were given permission to raise the fares. Foot passengers paid twopence instead of a penny and cars two shillings single or three shillings return. A lorry or van paid six shillings and a motor coach eight shillings and six pence single.

A FREE TRIP. The ferry was named *The Ivy* and on the first day that she crossed the river the children had a free trip, a half a days holiday from school, a penny and an orange. The two little girls who are leaning on the rails on the left are Mary and Joyce Hutchings. Their mother is waiting on the beach with their little sister, Margaret, in her arms.

A NEW DESIGN. A second Phillips ferry was brought into service in 1926. These ferries were much the same basic construction as the previous ones except that the traffic deck was now in the centre with the passenger accommodation and the boiler and engine rooms on either side. The reason for the change was the difficulty experienced in landing the traffic decks square onto the beach when there were strong winds or tides.

BEACH EXTENSION. Land adjoining the ferry slipways was bought to extend the beaches southwards on both sides of the river in 1929. This was to provide space for a second line of chains so that a double ferry service could be introduced. The work took two years to complete, from 1930 to 1932. Extra space on the roadside was also needed so the Ferry Hotel, in the centre of this photograph, was demolished. It had been an inn from 1793 to the 1920s and then was bought by Mr Fredman and turned into apartments.

DEMOLITION. The cottages to the right of the Ferry Hotel were also demolished. The building with the high-pitched roof was the police station. It was badly damaged in the Blitz of 1941. The police moved into the new ferry offices, which were built on the site of the cottages.

SLIPWAY UNDER CONSTRUCTION. The reconstruction work was done by a firm from Cardiff. This photograph, taken part way through the project, shows the gasworks. It was said to be among the last hand-charged plants in Britain and operated until 1969. The cottage nearby was occupied by Mr Godel, the man in charge of the gas enterprise. The other cottages lined Ferry Street. Many of them were badly damaged in the Blitz and had to be demolished. Many families had resided there, including England, Court, Pidgen, Johnson and Saxton.

FERRY GATES. Pedestrian tolls were collected on the Cornish side of the river. These are the old gates on the Torpoint side through which all vehicles passed. The small 'sentry-box' is the gatekeeper's booth.

TOLL HOUSE. With the reconstruction of the ferry beach, gantries, waiting rooms, a control house, ferry offices and a toll house were built of Cornish granite and Plymouth limestone. These are the waiting rooms on the Torpoint side with the turnstiles in the centre. The collectors sat in booths on either side of the turnstiles. One gantry, which housed the weights and chain mechanism can be seen on the left. The chains in the foreground are new ones waiting to be installed.

DOCK 'YARDIES' RUSHING TO WORK. There was rarely much spare room on the ferries which left Torpoint at 6.30a.m. and returned at 4.15p.m. The hundreds of men who worked in the dockyard crowded onto the traffic deck as well as all the passenger accommodation.

Two
Around the Town

Compared with its neighbours, Torpoint is a 'new town'. Its beginnings go back to the mid-1730s when, due to the fact that England seemed to be quarrelling with most of Europe and America, it was decided to expand the King's Dockyard at Plymouth. The chosen site was on the eastern bank of the Tamar as the land was, for the most part, uninhabited. It was also rather isolated from the small town of Plymouth, due to marshland and a lack of roads. The first workers were housed in hulks in the river but, not unnaturally, they wanted their families with them. The western bank of the river seemed to offer a solution to the problem so, with the help of the local landowners, the Pole Carews of Antony, Torpoint came into existence. By 1774 plans for the development of the town had been drawn up and were quite farsighted for their time. Commerce and industry flourished with both shopping and residential development being strictly controlled by the Estate. The 'old town' is still basically the same as it was in the 1800s. Fore Street, in particular, is little changed, except for shop front modifications, from its look of a hundred years ago, as can be seen in many of the photographs.

FORE STREET. A group of young people in a view captured for prosperity by A.J. Collings.

HILLSBOROUGH TERRACE. This was built just before the turn of the century and was the entrance to Torpoint. Little has changed there except that the pavements are not as high above the road as they were, due to layers of tarmac which have been laid down over the years. The road surface here, in the early years of the century, was earthen. The pillar box has now been moved to the higher side of Well Park Road, turning off to the left. The shop on the left was run by Mr Alfred Browning through the years up to the 1920s. It has also been; Blooms, Naval Tailors and, most recently, Gibson's opticians.

POTTERY ROAD. This is what it was originally known as in the last century. It ran alongside the water's edge from Carew Wharf to Carbeile Road. Its name was changed to Union Road and lastly to Marine Drive. The foreground has changed very little over the years. The first terrace on the right was Harbour View and the second Alexandra Terrace. The houses in the distance were known as Chapeldown Terrace. Now, all the houses are part of Marine Drive. The building behind the trees was the St Germans Union, which gave the road its second name.

THE ST GERMANS UNION. This was often referred to as the Workhouse and was an imposing building at the western end of Union Road. It was established in 1839 as the first in Cornwall to house paupers of various categories from the St Germans area. (The Board of Governors were responsible for the provision of minimum aid against starvation and homelessness for all in their area). The institution had a master, a matron a schoolmistress and porters amongst its staff. The population rose to over two hundred. A very sad aspect of the regulations governing its running was that, on entry, men were housed in one area and women in another which, being strictly adhered to, meant that husbands and wives were separated at a very fraught time in their lives. The Union was closed in 1940. The building gradually fell into decay and was demolished in 1963 and blocks of maisonettes built on the site.

THE ELLIS MONUMENT. This was erected in 1898 as a memorial to Benjamin James Ellis a thirty-six year old Torpoint man. On 19 July 1897 he was working in his garden at Barbadoes Cottages, before returning to his ship, HMS Cambridge, when he heard that three boys were in trouble. They had got into difficulties whilst swimming off the Ballast Pond. Still clad in his gardening clothes he swam to their rescue. Unfortunately Mr Ellis lost his life whilst saving the boys and public subscription erected the monument in his honour. Below the cross was a drinking fountain through which water flowed, then to a cattle trough, a further one for dogs and sheep and then into a sluice system.

SPARROW PARK. The Ellis monument was later enclosed in a walled park. A newspaper man reporting the ceremony commented, 'Call that a park; it's only fit for sparrows!' and the name stuck. The large drinking trough which had been attached to the monument was later sited on the pavement. The large pseudo-Tudor house in the background, Udal Garth, was built in 1897 for Dr Sidney Vinter. He was a general practitioner in the town from the 1890s to the 1920s.

COMRADES' CLUB. The Torpoint Comrades and United Services' Club was opened in these two huts, in Antony Road, by Lady Beatrice Pole Carew on 22 October 1920. The huts had been purchased from the army at Tregantle. One hut was used for meetings and the other for social events such as parties, dances, billiards and band practice. When the club was opened the minutes recorded that bass and bitter were to be eight pence a pint and whisky sixpence ha'penny a 'drop'. On the opposite side of the road were allotments and the site of the present club which was opened in 1953. Beyond is Albion Road school.

24

ALBION ROAD SCHOOL. Built in 1910, it first housed the infants from the Wesleyan school in Macey Street and the boys and infants from the National school. The National school, opened in 1823, was overcrowded and it was practical to begin to gather all the town's school children together under one roof. The juniors and seniors from Macey Street amalgamated with the Council school in Albion Road on 2 October 1922. Albion Road housed the infant, junior and senior schools until 1954 when a new junior school was built at Carbeile and later a new secondary school was opened in 1963. This school is now the Torpoint infants' school.

MOUNT EDGCUMBE TERRACE. This was built on the western edge of the town in what was known as Carbeile Estate sometime around 1898. It was a terrace of fine houses overlooking St John's Lake and Mount Edgcumbe. Immediately in front of it and to the rear were fields and allotments. In the late 1940s, prefabs were built to accommodate families who had lost homes through the Blitz and those whose menfolk had returned from the services. In the 1950s and 1960s a large housing estate was built behind the terrace.

THE LAWN. This was a favourite spot for the people of Torpoint and, indeed, for many from Devonport. Weekends would see the area crowded with families who spent half a day or even a whole day there. It has been said that, in the 1930s, if you weren't there by ten o' clock on a Sunday, you would have difficulty in finding a suitable place to sit. The wooded area led up to what had been the grounds of Thanckes House.

RECREATION LAWN. This is the description given to the area by local photographer A.J.Collings. Swimming was a favourite occupation. A large area had been walled off to form a swimming pool, often known as Horseshoe Lake. A sluice in the riverside wall could be opened and closed to regulate and refresh the flow of water.

THE LAWN. The swimming pool can be seen clearly here. The circular structure is the base of the bandstand where local bands entertained the townsfolk in the first forty years of this century. The tea hut was a very popular addition to the Lawn, operated over the years by members of the Banks and Pearson families. Away to the left was a quarry where a miniature rifle range was opened in July 1909.

TORPOINT CASTLE was the name given by local people to this folly built in the grounds of Gravesend House by Admiral Henry Harrison, who was the port admiral of Plymouth in the middle of the eighteenth century. He built Gravesend House in the 1750s on land previously owned by Lord Graves, of Thanckes House. He had enough building material left to erect this building as a summer house. It has now been demolished.

THE INSTITUTE. This was a very imposing building in Tamar Street. It had a hall and meeting rooms and was used for dances, meetings of the Literary Society, dinners and lectures. It also had a reading room. A gallery ran around the main hall and many of the older people of the town can remember when mothers, seated up in the gallery, kept a watchful eye on their daughters dancing below. The building suffered bomb damage in 1941 and the cost of renovating it after the War proved prohibitive. The horse outside is probably drawing a water cart used to damp the dusty streets. The high-pitched roof in the background belonged to the police station and the road past it ran to the ferry. The shop belonging to a baker called John Snell can also be seen. The building on the right is East Cornwall House.

EAST CORNWALL HOUSE, mid-1920s. This house stood on the corner of Tamar and Fore Streets. For nearly fifty years in the last century it was the location of Down Bros. shop. They were chemists, tea dealers, grocers, linen and woollen drapers, stationers and insurance agents. At the time this photograph was taken, the shops were a drapers, Oatway's ironmongers, Hosking's fruiterers and Alford's grocers. Later Mr Hosking ran a taxi business, the Misses Drew ran refreshment rooms and Mr Kent's drapery was in the shop on the right. Prior to 1937, the Torpoint Urban District Council held its meetings in rooms on the first floor of the building. On Friday evenings books from the county library could be exchanged in a room there. In 1941 the building was partly demolished by a near miss which tore away that part of the building on the corner of Macey and Tamar Streets. The remainder of East Cornwall House was repaired and used, up until it was demolished in the late 1960s to provide a car park.

THE FACTORY. The artist has used a fair amount of licence in his representation of the buildings at what is now known as Carew Wharf. The original factory was built for Joshua Rowe's rope and varnish manufactory in the 1790s. In 1853 Messrs Eastcott and Shepheard built their Western Counties Manure Factory. They produced sulphuric acid and fertiliser. That enterprise was ended in 1914 when the premises were gutted by fire. In 1925 Reynolds Bros. bought it and it became the Torpoint and District General Supply Company, operating as coal, agricultural and builders' merchants. The tall chimney gradually became dangerous; the top was removed in 1923 and the base in 1930.

THE TOP OF FORE STREET, sometime between 1898 and 1912. The Ellis memorial was already in place and there was a gas street lamp. This lamp, known as the three-lighter because of the three gas lights in it, was presented to the town by Captain Reginald Pole Carew on his return from the Afghan campaign. It was erected here in what was known as the Box-heater because of its triangular shape. It was moved twice before 1912 when the council moved it to its present position in Eliot Square. The large building beyond the lamp became the post office in 1913. The houses on the immediate left, Clarence Place, must be among the oldest still in the town.

ST JAMES CHURCH. This was built as a chapel of ease to the parish church at Antony. The first service was held on Easter day in 1819. It eventually became a parish church in 1872. The tree-lined road on the right has been variously known as Tree Hill, The Avenue and now Salamanca Road. The original trees were blown down in a severe storm in the late 1920s and the present ones were planted by school children in 1937.

THE EAST END OF ST JAMES CHURCH. The church was built to seat five hundred people. A gallery on three sides was planned to have rented pews as it was thought, by the Revd Duke Yonge, that the wealthier residents of the town would take these and therefore take a greater interest in the church. The original musical accompaniment was a cello. An organ was not introduced until the turn of the century. In 1886 the church was extended eastwards with the addition of a chancel when the style was Early English. The old turret was removed and a new one of oak with a slate roof substituted. It housed a clock subscribed for by parishioners. On the left of the photograph is Salamanca House which was once a private school and on the right the shops of Eliot Square. The building in the background is the National school.

BUILDING REGULATIONS. When Torpoint's Fore Street was in the planning stage in the 1770s, Reginald Pole Carew, the landowner, laid down strict rules for the buildings. They were to be of stone (from his nearby quarry) or brick and built in a straight line three storeys in height. 'Footways' each side of the street were to be six feet wide, paved with a flat pavement. No portico, bow window, signpost or projection was to be erected next to the street. Some changes have been made in the last two hundred years but the Fore Street of the past can still be recognised as the busy shopping street of today. Mr Oatway is no longer selling Pratt's Spirit, and barbers Palmer and Toms have long since gone. In their place are now Trobridge, the solicitors, and The Coffee Pot. Tailor Coaker had been in his shop on the left for twenty years at the time of this photograph and would have been very familiar with all the delivery carts. The Co-op is now on that spot and has to have all its deliveries made at the rear of the premises.

FORE STREET, 1935. The shop on the left was Edward King's butchers and next door was the bakers which had been run by the Granger family since 1873. Now the butcher is Roger Harvey and the bakers premise is a Chinese take-away. At the start of the next block is the Wheeler's Hotel, which was originally called the New Inn in the 1830s. The Wheeler family were licencees until 1891 and in 1867 they changed the name to Wheeler's New Inn. At the time of the photograph George Crinks was licencee. Alongside was Veal's bakers and then the Co-op. The pillarbox on the right stood outside East Cornwall House. The next block had Mrs Beaver's fruiterers, now a newsagents, and a sweetshop run by Mrs Elizabeth Banks, which is now a solicitors.

31

LOOKING FROM GRAVESEND, 1913. This is the view of one of the oldest parts of Torpoint seen from the grounds of Gravesend House which was built in the 1750s. The rear of the houses in Fore Street and Macey Street can be seen. The tall building is the Methodist chapel, built in 1795. The cottages on the water's edge by the boats are in Kings Terrace. Beyond this is Windsor Terrace and the pontoon can be seen running out into the river. Beyond are some of the naval ships alongside the dockyard.

LOW TIDE. Boats are moored in front of Kings Terrace. Beyond the washing line are the houses in King Street and to the left Windsor Terrace. The building to the right is the Methodist chapel.

LOOKING DOWN FORE STREET. This is a view of the lower part of Fore Street in the early years of this century. The corner shop on the left was a grocer's owned by Mr Fred Stivey and his immediate neighbour with the two boys standing outside was the Jubilee Inn, whose licensee was James Williams. Alongside was Thomas Reynolds' bakers shop. Shortly after this photograph was taken this building had pinnacles placed over the second floor windows. This is now Slee's butchers shop. Further down the street was Thomas Stacey's bootmakers premises, now a travel agent, and the barber's shop which was in the Toms family for over forty years. The shop on the right hand corner was run by the Gosling family who had grocers shops in Fore Street for over sixty years. Now it is Williams' chemists.

PARK AND RIDE. This was the scene in the car park of Chalk's garage in Antony Road on 10 October 1936. Plymouth Argyle supporters had left their cars here before travelling to Home Park for the cup match against Aston Villa. The result was a draw, two goals each. The proprietor of the garage at this time was Mr H. Redwood. Beyond the cars can be seen the Folly at Gravesend.

BARRAGE BALLOON. After some detective work, the authors are led to believe that this photograph was taken just prior to the Second World War. It is thought that the barrage balloon was part of a recruiting drive on behalf of the Royal Air Force. It is being raised in the car park of Chalk's garage in Antony Road. The facts which point to a date before the War are: no gas masks or tin helmets carried by policeman or civilians, normal registration plates on lorries (service vehicles in wartime had 'special' numbers), no masks on vehicle headlights and the sailor has a white cap top, these were suspended during the war.

THANCKES HOUSE. Pengelly House was the first built on this site in around 1300. The second Thanckes House, built in 1714, was pulled down in 1870 and this one built in 1871. It was built by Lord Graves, whose family had inherited the previous house. It stood in large grounds on a site to the north of the present bowling green. About the turn of this century the house passed to the Pole Carews. It is thought that, as Torpoint was expanding towards Thanckes, it became increasingly difficult to let it as a country house. A hotel and a riding stable had not proved profitable. It was sold to a Plymouth syndicate and transferred stone by stone to Portwrinkle to open in 1911 as the Whitsand Bay Hotel.

Three
Churches, Chapels and Ministers

Religion was a long time arriving in the town of Torpoint or, at least, it was all of fifty years before its first church was built. John Wesley, on one of his visits to Dock, or as we know it, Devonport, recorded in his journal, ' I was desired to go over to Torpoint, a village on the Cornish side of the water, I am in hopes a plentiful harvest will spring from the seed which was sown this hour.' It was after this visit that several worthies joined with some in Devonport to build the first place of worship in Torpoint. Prior to this, all religious services had to take place at Antony, three miles away. In 1795 Methodists were settled in Torpoint, in 1810 the Congregationalists opened their church in Rowe Street. Before that date they had been licensed to meet in houses of members throughout the town. With the increase in Non-conformity the establishment and the Anglicans were a little worried and so the Pole Carew family sanctioned the building of a chapel of ease in the town. In 1872 this became the parish church of St James. The Roman Catholics had to wait until 1933 for their church of St Joan of Arc to be built. The other major event in the religious life of the town was the opening of the cemetery at Horson in 1928. Prior to this date all burials took place at Antony, a long walk on a wet and windy winter's day!

DECORATIVE PLAQUE. This was situated over the Methodist church doorway.

JOHN WESLEY. He preached in Torpoint at 1.15 p.m. on 2 March 1787. He wrote in his journal that he 'believed the large number of people who listened attentively had not heard in vain'. His belief was well founded as Methodism took root in Torpoint. This chapel in Fore Street was opened in 1795. The gentleman standing on the corner was 'Johnno'. For many years he stood on that spot and sold ice cream in the summer and hot chestnuts in the winter.

INTERIOR OF METHODIST CHAPEL. In 1909 Joseph Shepherd bought the adjoining house and gave it to the Methodists to extend the chapel. A vestry was added and a beautiful memorial stained glass window was installed. In later years a new organ was purchased and the front of the chapel was altered. This photograph is as most people will have remembered the chapel from the 1930s until its demise. Methodists worshipped here until 1987 when the building was considered unsafe. They joined with the United Reformed church to become Cornerstone. Plans are now under way to renovate the building.

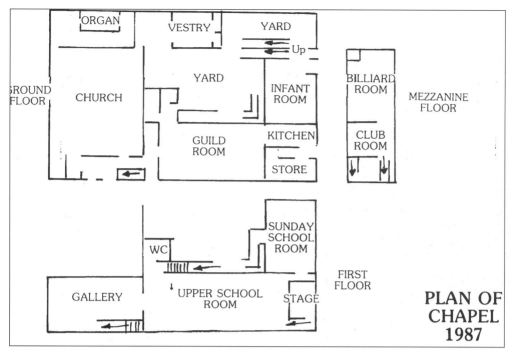

Plan labels: ORGAN, VESTRY, YARD, Up, GROUND FLOOR, CHURCH, YARD, INFANT ROOM, BILLIARD ROOM, MEZZANINE FLOOR, GUILD ROOM, KITCHEN, CLUB ROOM, STORE, WC, SUNDAY SCHOOL ROOM, FIRST FLOOR, GALLERY, UPPER SCHOOL ROOM, STAGE

PLAN OF CHAPEL 1987

THE CHAPEL. This had a social as well as a religious side. Over the years there were flourishing groups for the young people. Plays and concerts provided entertainment in the upper rooms as the plan shows. During the last war some of the rooms were used as a forces canteen.

ST JAMES CHURCH. Between 1800 and 1810 the population of Torpoint increased by 50 per cent; the only places of worship in the town were non-conformist. Anglicans had to travel three miles to Antony for services and this distance was too far for young children and the elderly. The answer to this problem was to build a chapel of ease in Torpoint. It was built on land sold by Mr John Smith to the Right Honourable Reginald Pole Carew. The first service was held in the church of St James the Great on Easter day in 1819. In 1872 it became a parish church with the Revd Edgar Huxtable as vicar.

THE EAST END OF ST JAMES. The new chancel was added to the church in 1885. In the months that the work was carried out services were held in the Good Templars' Hall (this building is now the St John's Ambulance Hall). The first service in the extended church was conducted by the Bishop of Truro on 13 July 1886. In 1935 another major reconstruction took place when the side galleries and the lower windows were removed.

BIBLE CHRISTIAN CHAPEL. This group were active in Torpoint from 1827. At first they held their meetings in the premises of a local carrier, Mr Crart; later in the first floor rooms at No.39 Fore Street. They built their first church in Macey Street. In 1905 it became the Foresters' Hall, now the Conservative Club. The Bible Christians built the chapel in this photograph on the corner of York and Buller Roads in 1905. When they united with the Wesleyans, the chapel was sold to the Urban District Council. It was extended and opened as their offices in 1937 and is still the Council Hall.

THE CATHOLIC CHURCH. This was situated in Modder Road. For many years the nearest church for the Catholics in Torpoint was at Mutton Cove, Devonport or Plymouth. They had to walk each way and this often meant leaving home at 7.15 a.m. As more Catholics came to live in the area a priest came to hold mass in Catholic homes. The first mass in the town was held at Easter in 1914 in a house in Sydney Road. Eventually a collection was started to raise sufficient funds to build a Catholic church in Torpoint. In November 1932 the foundation stone of the church was laid by Bishop Barrett.

SIMPLE YET BEAUTIFUL. The Catholic church, when opened, had only a wooden floor with a square of red carpet in the sanctuary. One hundred second-hand wooden chairs and a well-worn harmonium were purchased yet all exceeded the dreams of the parishioners. On the wall at the back hung a crucifix presented to the church by a British soldier. It was found on the battlefield during the Battle of the Somme. The interior is much changed now.

St. Joan of Arc,
Modder Road,
Torpoint.

❖⟫○⟪❖

SOUVENIR OF
laying the Foundation Stone of
her New Church by
His Lordship, Bishop Barrett,
on
Sunday, 27th November, 1932.

❖⟫○⟪❖

Clients and Parishioners should show their love of St. Joan of Arc by contributing generously to the building and upkeep of this Outpost of the Faith in Cornwall.

❖⟫○⟪❖

Canon Burke will receive your offerings and acknowledge them with gratitude.

ST JOAN OF ARC. Bishop Barrett had attended the canonisation of St Joan of Arc in Rome in May 1920 and he promised that the next church he built in the Plymouth diocese would be dedicated to her, and that church happened to be in Torpoint. It was opened in March 1933. The presbytery alongside was built in 1938 and the first resident priest was Father John Delaney.

PARISH PRIEST. Father Joseph Elwell served the church of St Joan of Arc from 1944 to 1948.

FIRST COMMUNICANTS. These children made their First Communion at St Joan of Arc on Low Sunday in 1936. Back row: Kevin Britton, Mary Hanrahan, Madge Power, Pat Carter, Pat Power. Front row: -?-, Francis Crocker, -?-, -?-.

MONTY MAY. The Revd George Montague May was ordained in 1883. He began his career in the church of the Holy Trinity, Plymouth and later in Keyham. He came to Torpoint after being the vicar of Chittlehampton in North Devon. He took up his duties in Torpoint in July 1911 and so began a lively, energetic and sometimes controversial incumbency of seventeen years. Known then and for many years afterwards as 'Monty' he made a very deep impression on the town and its people.

THE REVD HOWARD MILES BROWN. Born in London and moving to Saltash at the age of eleven, Miles Brown started his working life in the Plymouth City Engineer's office. In 1938 he began to train for the priesthood and was ordained in 1940. In 1942 he returned to Cornwall and was appointed assistant curate in Calstock. He came to Torpoint, his first parish, in 1946. He spent six years here and then moved to St Paul's, Truro. He was a formidable scholar who wrote many books marking his lifelong interest in Cornish churches, history and clocks. He was a clockmaker and organ builder.

THE REVD ALFRED BISHOP. He came to Torpoint Methodist chapel in 1898 as a lay agent (now known as a pastor). He had applied to become a missionary but his health did not permit it. He was ordained as a minister in 1903. He was remembered with great affection for many years after his death in 1912.

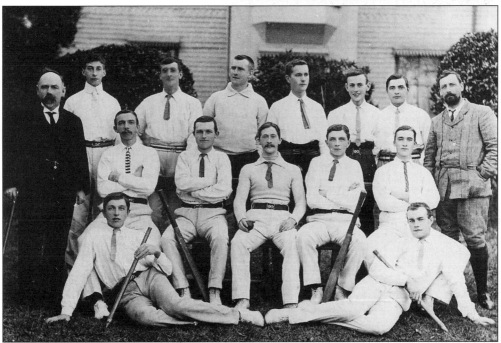

WESLEY CRICKET TEAM, 1906. Back row: W. Hancock, Ern Perry, Jack Coaker, E. Hayman, E. Selley, E. Bersey. Middle row: J.E. Reynolds Esq, W. Cropp, A.C. Collins, D.B. Peacock, H. Northmore, F. Roberts, Mr W. Collins R.N. Front row: Henry Northmore, R. Andrew.

REVD CHARLES KENNERLY, the vicar of Torpoint from 1901 to 1911. Here he is seen with the St James A.F.C. team, who, in the 1903-4 season won seventeen of their twenty-one matches with ninety-three goals for and eighteen against. Back row: T. Wakeham, R. Hall, S. Snell, R. Walters. Middle row: D. Sammels, A. Perkins, Revd C. Kennerly, E. Hayman, F. Palmer. Front row: A.J. Kent, J. Williams, C. Dawe (captain), A. Prideaux, R. Macey.

ST JAMES A.F.C. 1919-1920. Back row: P. Cudlip, C. Nodder, S. Glover, A. McCreery, J. Hancock, J. Parnow, A. Williams, G. Webster, L. Chard, C. Hannaford, Middle row: G. Cocking, E. Cocks, J. Tabb, J. Cocks (chairman) A. Wadge, R. Hambly, J. Osborn. Front row: G. Paul, C. Parker, E. Bull, S. Paul, J. Bowen.

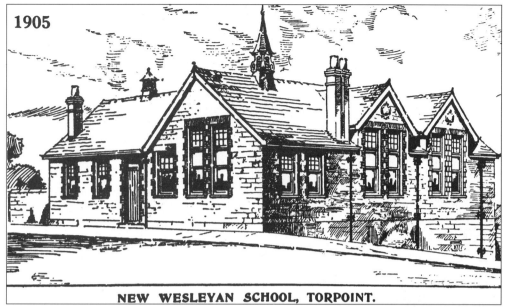

1905

NEW WESLEYAN SCHOOL, TORPOINT.

WESLEYAN SCHOOL, which opened in 1841 in the rooms attached to the chapel. By 1904 they had become so overcrowded that a new school was built just down the hill. At a cost of £2,200 Macey Street school was built to accommodate one hundred and fifty children and opened in February 1905. Until education became free for all children the pupils here paid a penny a week. The school was used until 1964, in later years as an outpost of the local secondary school.

FESTIVAL WINNERS, 1951. Young people from the Methodist chapel took part in the annual Plymouth Methodist festival. Some of the certificate winners are seen here with their Minister Revd John Myer. Back row: Enid Williams, Colin Murch, June Clarke, Ruth Hyslop, Murray Hyslop, Ron Mallett, Sylvia Squance. Front row: Janice Beaton, Ruth Ellison, Marlene Godfrey, Revd John Myer, Cyril Bunney.

MONTY'S GUARDS. During the First World War Revd Monty May began an organisation for lads in the town. It provided youth activities at a time when many fathers were away in the armed forces or working long hours in the Dockyard. It was run like a cadet corps with half a dozen young men from the church helping the vicar. They wore a navy uniform with red piping and peaked caps. They had summer camps at Looe, Paignton and Teignmouth, where they were billeted for the week in church halls. The fife and drum band led the Guards in many parades all round the district and to the church services at Antony, St John and Plymouth. The bandmaster was Mr Bill Peach. The young gentleman in khaki was Albert Fellows, home on leave from the army.

GIRLS LOYALTY GUARDS. Miss Rhoda May formed a branch of the Loyalty Guards for girls. Amongst other activities they had their own band and attended camp. Back row: Elsie Tamblyn, Eileen Trotman, Dorothy Chalice. Middle row: Dorothy Adams, Ethel Rouse, Phyllis King, Lena Giddy. Front row: Vera Soden, Vera Clarke.

CHURCH LOYALTY GUARDS (MONTY'S GUARDS). Back row: Tommy Riddle, Bert Prideaux, Len Squance, Bill Snell, Bob Tweedie, Gerry Gorman, Arthur Johnson, David Cockerill, Ted Perkins, Fred Pearce, Frank Woodman, Henry Pigden, Norma Morgan. Third row: Bill Peach, Bill Bailey, Charlie Clunn, Stan Jones, Fred Gobey, Ken Jordan, George Cater, Ern Tippett, Charlie Leach, Roy Morgan, George Mudge, Edgar Pearson, Cecil Pearson, Cecil Chard, T. Brocking, Ted Brooking, Ted Curwood, Bill Knott. Second row: Mrs White, Miss Rhoda May, Charlie Humpherson, R. Marks, Alec Hines, Revd Monty May, Mr Wright, Mr Jordan, Mrs Hines, Mrs Hoyle. Front row: includes Tom Hoyle, Bill Wevill, Albert England.

THE METHODIST CHOIR was augmented by friends to perform *The Galilean* in 1968 to celebrate the one hundred and seventy third anniversary of the chapel. The Choir included Messrs John Bullock, Lock, Jewell, Ken Eddy, Mesdames Martin, Williams, Sullivan, Duncan, Jewell, Shears, J. Horton, Andrews, Stone, Cross, Friend, Miss E. Parker, Miss J. Beaver, Mesdames Woolcock, Bates, Killick, Redding, Messrs W. Hoare, Lee, S. Olufsen, Mesdames, Deacon, Kawalski, H. Horton, Trudgeon, D. Madge, J. Sandford, Messrs L. Andrew, J. Hyslop, H. Sandford. Soloists were Frank Soden, Geoff Oatey and the conductor was Mr Barry Deacon.

CHOIR OF ST JAMES CHURCH, 1920s. Back row: Jack Lock, Arthur Youings, D.W. Jones, Jimmy Veal, Ralph Grinter, Alan Shearman, Ted Eustace. Third row: David Cockwell, Mr Lock, Charlie Routley, Cyril Gorman, Ted Short, Sid Eustace, Clarrie Eustace, Roy Morgan, -?-. Second row: Freddie Ellis, Stuart Collins, Revd Monty May, William Hurden, Alec Hines. Front row: Wilfred Rundle, Bill Lock , Edmund Rundle.

THE CONGREGATIONAL CHURCH BAND, 1923. Only a few members have been identified: The middle row includes: Tommy Walters, Percy Sleep, 'Pa' Jordan, Stuart Sleep, George Williams, W.Tyler. The front row includes: Fred Prideaux, J. Hancock, Tom Soady.

REVD BERNARD LOWE was vicar of Torpoint from 1932 to 1946. He was very much involved in the major construction work done in the 1930s. There is a stone set into one of the buttresses on the north wall of the church commemorating him, with the inscription 'B.S.L. 1935'. Here he is seen in the vicarage garden with his senior staff. Standing: William Jope (churchwarden), Clifford Palmer, Francis Hill, J.F. Williams (churchwarden). Seated: Ernest Grinter, Revd Bernard Lowe, Gerald Cocking.

YOUNG MEN'S CHRISTIAN FELLOWSHIP, 1934. This was conducted by Revd Bernard Lowe which attracted many. Back row: Frank Ratcliffe, Harold Gorman, Kenneth Hall, Charles Waters, -?-, -?-, Victor Gorman. Third row. Charles Ratcliffe, Henry Bowen, Stanley Memory, John Porter, John Bowen, Felix Grinter. Seated: -?- Bert Bremyer, Revd Bernard Lowe, Arthur Hancock, Francis Geray. Front row: Arthur Hingston, Gwynne Skyrme, David Willcocks, James Ellis, Roy Gilbert.

Four
Sport

Sport was always a great leisure occupation in the town, although, in keeping with the times, it seemed to be mostly for the male population. The exceptions were hockey, tennis and rowing in which there were local teams ready to give a good account of themselves. The male sports were generally based on the churches, pubs and clubs and covered rowing, sailing, tug-of-war, cricket, football, bowls and rifle-shooting and, for many of these sports the teams of Torpoint were reckoned to be among the best in Cornwall and Devon.

THE YOUNG ROD. These rowers were winners of the Watson Cup for the under nineteen's, at the Torpoint Regatta in September 1921.

THE TORPOINT ROWING CLUB. This was originally called the Torpoint Athletic Rowing Club. Many of the men of Torpoint spent a large part of their lives on the water in one way or another so it seemed a natural development to form a club. They were used to rowing thirty-two foot gigs and they often took them on picnic trips up the river. After the First World War Harry Gilbert and Ernie Greet were amongst those who formed the Rowing Club. They each put up £12 10s cash to buy the *Jesse Esther* and another gig to use in races. The *Jesse Esther* was kept in the stables of the Ferry Hotel. The *Rodney* was bought from the 'Essa' club at Saltash. Before long Torpoint had become a name to be feared in the rowing world. These are the rowers who won first prize in the race for six-oared gigs open to the Port of Plymouth in 1921. These are Stanley Budge, W. Butson, D. Hambly, Ed Bawden, Norman Rickard, George Furzland and R. Williams.

BEWARE OF THE WASPS, 1925. The ladies formed their own team and called themselves The Wasps. The Budge sisters were stalwart members of the team.

A GIG IN THE 1930s. Jim Palmer, the cox, is holding the trophies this team have won. With him are Reg Butson, Steve Hannaford, Bill Knott, Cyril Hannaford, Vernon Eddy and Arthur Pearce. The club bought two, sixty foot huts. One was erected at Thanckes football field and the other was used for boat storage at the bottom of Quarry Street. For many years the club had its headquarters in the East Cornwall Wines and Spirits Vaults (now the Trot Inn).

TORPOINT WAS A NAME TO BE FEARED. Evidence of this is seen in the array of trophies shown here. The rowers also look a formidable lot and were 'Champions of the Tamar' in 1927-28. Back row: Frank Freathy, Tom Cross, Bill Court, Bill Stroud, 'Neebo' Lance. Middle row: Ern Clemas, George Lavers, Charlie Welsh, Wilfred Hannaford, Ed Clemas, Jim (Bobby) Rickard. Front row: Alf Dingle, Jerry Harvey, Bill Thompson, George Hoyle, Jim Hambly.

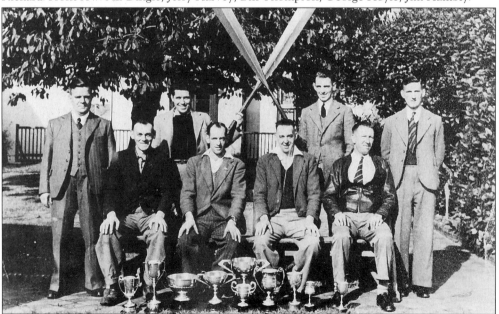

A NEW START. The club folded in 1935 but had a new lease of life in the early 1950s, and once again, collected the trophies. Back row: Albert Stroud, -?-, -?-, Arthur Pearce. Front row: Vic Searle, Alfred Kinsman, Phil Ackland, Bill Knott.

RIFLE SHOOTING. This had its roots in Torpoint as far back as the 1870s, but the Miniature Rifle Club was formed at an inaugural meeting in the Wesleyan schoolroom in 1907. The first club range was on land in the grounds of Thanckes House, in the old quarry, offered by Sir Reginald Pole Carew at an annual rent of one shilling, provided the members did all the necessary work. The range was opened on 19 July 1909 by Lady Beatrice Pole Carew. Sir Reginald said he had no idea the place could be made so charming and imagined there was no better range to be found in the West of England.

TROPHY TABLE, 1912. The members of the club shown with their trophies include, back row: Wm. McKim, George Devonshire, Harry Frost, Dr Thomas, C. Schofield, James Wiltshire, E. Woolley, A. Clive, F. James. Middle row: George Westlake, Amos Sleeman, J.Wood, W. Trevithick, A. James, Lewis Hancock, R. Beaumont, Arthur Devonshire, Bertram Norgate. On 27 May they won the Buchanan Trophy against all England and Wales, in 1913 the Three Towns Outdoor Shield, the Mt Edgcumbe Cup and the Inter Counties Bowl, at Tavistock.

CORNISH CHAMPIONS. The club (which had between forty and fifty members at its opening) competed against teams from Antony, St Budeaux, R.N. Barracks and others in the Plymouth area. In their first year of competition they won the Cornish Championship with the team of Arthur Devonshire, R.H. Beaumont, F.G. Jeffries and Amos Sleeman.

TRIUMPH IN WALES, 1912. The team travelled to Wales and returned with the Dragon Championship Trophy. Back row: R. Beaumont , W. Trevithick. Front row: Amos Sleeman, Arthur Devonshire.

ONE HUNDRED AND EIGHTY. As in all towns darts has long been one of the favoured games in the local clubs and public houses. Seen here is the team from the Conservative and Unionist club with their trophies. Back row: Bill Harris, 'Dasher' Rice, Fred Rogers, Frank Searle, Eric Carter, Ivor Dawe, Bill Dawe. Front row: Horace Devonshire, Charlie Nodder, Fred Gliddon, Joe Lobb, Sid Johnson.

TENNIS was played on courts at Gravesend and Thanckes. Each venue had its own team and there were matches between them. This is the Thanckes team of the 1920s. Back row: Ern Perry, Robert Hambly, W. Black, H. Short, Ernest Cocks. Middle row: Stan Squires, Mrs B. Squires, Mrs A. Smith, Mark Bray, Mrs D. Short, Mrs W. Hambly, Leslie Squires. Front row: Mrs G. Reep, Mrs Marjorie Blackler.

TORPOINT BOWLING CLUB. In 1923 a local businessman, Mr White, gathered a group of interested people with the idea of forming a bowling club. The founder members included Messrs William Rose, William Turner, Jack Coaker, Henry Evans, Harry Freathy and James Wiltshire. The green is on the site of the old Thanckes House. It was presented to the town by Sir Reginald Pole Carew and was opened by Major G.C. Ellers, on behalf of Sir Reginald in 1924. The first match was against Tothill Park and the first cup competition against Saltash, which Torpoint won by two shots.

BOWLS CHAMPIONS, 1934. In this year the Torpoint Bowling Club won the championship of the first division of the Plymouth & District Bowling League. It has been recalled that in order to win the championship the team had to win the last two matches away from home to win on shot average which, of course, they did. Back row: Dave Greeno, Reg Cudlip, J. Osborne, -?-, Johnny Bradford, -?-. Middle row: Revd Bernard Lowe, Lt. Cdr. Broom, Mr Worrall, Mr Hayman, Mark Bennett, Mr Harris, D.B. Peacock, W. Bayliss, Mr Sibley. Front row: Harry Freathy, Lt. Cdr. Turner, Mr Farmer, Lt. Cdr. Grinter, Lt. Cdr. Griffin, Tom Morley.

SAILING CLUB. The Torpoint Mosquito Sailing Club was formed in 1891. Three of the founder members were the Reep brothers. They had premises north of the ferry and a boat shed for the Mosquito class boats. Among the earlyboats were: *Irene* (belonging to: W.Harris); *Hornet* (T. Tambling); *Cygnet* (A.Trotman); *Lillian* (A. Reep); *Brittania* (W. Symons). Regattas were held regularly until 1899, then there was a gap until about 1913, when they restarted.

THE GNATS. In the 1930s a cadet branch of the Sailing Club was formed, called the Gnats. Three of the members were: Jim Broad, Hector Woodhouse, Roy Woodhouse. One of the boats they sailed was the *Clara*.

HEAVY TUG OF WAR TEAM. Many of the tug-of-war teams were also rowers and men who were used to heavy manual work. They trained by rigging heavy weights on shear legs and spent their lunch hours pulling. Their trainer, Frank Pritchard, had been a sergeant in the Royal Marines. The Royal Navy took tug-of-war seriously and Torpoint was invited to pull against a champion Navy team (whose trainer was a Torpoint man, Harry Leach). They pulled on two occasions and beat the Navy each time. The team included: Harry Leach, Arthur Knott, Bert Pritchard, Stan Warne, George Hoyle, George Osborne, Harry Downing, Ernie Clemas, Dan Glanville.

LIGHT TUG OF WAR TEAM. Back row: Sid Pearce, Arthur Knott, Albert Knott, George Osborne, Syd Hannaford, Dan Glanville, George Hoyle. Front row: Stan Warne, Harry Downing, Charlie Leach, Albert Ward, Paddy Connor.

CYCLE SPEEDWAY. In 1950 at a meeting at the Church House, it was decided that Torpoint should form a team to take part in the Plymouth and District Cycle Speedway League. Thus the Torpoint Flyers took off. The gentlemen behind its formation were Brian and Les Cardew, Dennis Conyon, Jack Kingston and Messrs Medlin and Crowle. Back row: George King, Jack Kingston, 'Fringe' Tippett, Ewart Grundy, Frank Horner. Front row: S. Paul, Raymond Williams, Eric Abbott, Arthur Paige, David Pearn.

THE SPEEDWAY TRACK. This was at the Mill, Torpoint. The crowd which came to watch the races was treble the soccer crowd. However, the club was, unfortunately, disbanded in 1953 because of lack of support, enthusiasm and competition.

SCHOOL ATHLETICS. These were very much to the fore in Torpoint in the 1950s and 60s. These winners were photographed sometime around 1950. Back row: Margaret Worth, Terry Haigh, Barry Weighill, Raymond Williams, Norman Bailey. Front row: Beryl Cardew, Barbara Dunstan, Ivona Williams.

HOCKEY. Ladies' and mixed hockey teams played in Torpoint in the 1920s. Games were played at the Mill. A few of the ladies in this photograph have been identified. The back row includes: May Ellison, Nellie Budge, Nellie Bawden, Amy Budge. The front row includes: Eileen Trotman, Kath Nethercott.

CRICKET. St James church had its first cricket team in 1899 and it played its first match against St James church, Keyham in June of that year. The match was played on ground at Borough Farm, lent by Mr Hancock. A year later at a public meeting in the Institute it was decided to form a cricket club in connection with Torpoint and district. The Torpoint Cricket Club has been functioning, with some breaks, since that time. Back row: Reg Smith, Jack Kingston, Bernard Wagg, Bill Dawe, Bill Davis, Ivor Dawe. Middle row: Fred Dawe, Cyril Paling, Mr Lines, Dick Wagg, Geoff Peach. Front row: 'Skipper' Griffin, Wyndham Bartley, Frank Bolton.

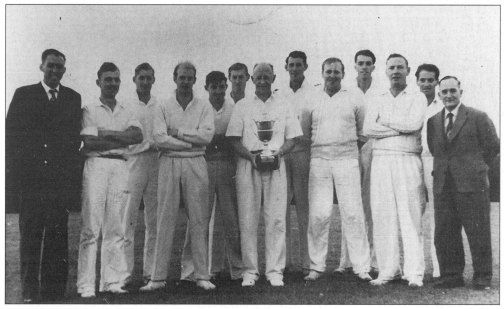

CRICKET, 1960s. Left to right: Jack Kingston, Gerry Broad, John Fugler, Dennis Harding, Ivor Dawe, Jim Callan, Bill Dawe, Bob Symons, Bruce Cudlip, Fred Dawe, David Lakeman.

TORPOINT ASSOCIATION FOOTBALL CLUB.

J. E. Coaker,   W. Hayman,   F. W. Roberts,   A. Northcott,   C. W. Reynolds,   S. W. Tabb,   E. Pe
A. B. Reynolds,   *(Captain.)*   W. J. R
(Hon. Sec.)   W. F. Reynolds,   F. Prideaux,   R. V. Goad,   L. F. Selley,   W. P. Coaker.   *(Hon. t*

TORPOINT HAS FIELDED MANY FOOTBALL TEAMS. Two of the earliest teams were the Defiance and the Triumph. In 1905 they were merged and a meeting on 15 August that year saw the birth of Torpoint Athletic Football Club. Its president was General Sir Reginald Pole Carew and the vice presidents included: Drs Chubb and Vinter, Revd Kennerley, Messrs T.E. Reynolds, W and J. Rose and H. Frost. They played on the Victoria Park pitch (now the site of Peacock Avenue). In the 1905-6 season they won the Cornwall Senior Cup, the Durning Lawrence Charity Cup and the Plymouth & District League. This photograph was taken in the garden of Dr Vinter's house, Udal Garth in May 1906. The goalkeeper's white sweater cost six shillings!

64

SUCCESS. This was repeated in the 1932-33 season when Torpoint Athletic again won the Cornwall Senior Cup. Back row: Frank Elliott, Stan Toms, Fred Barby, George Scantlebury, Arthur Quiller, Frank Collins, Bill Cross. Middle row: Ed Hancock, Les Grinter, Cyril Roberts, Jim Balsden, Ern Memory, George Osborne, Fred Prideaux, -?-, Roy Westlake, Harry Morris, Charlie Humpherson, ? Sparks. Front row: Dave Anning, Sam Cross, Fred Roberts, William Turner, Alfred Whiting, George Balke, Fred Lampen. The senior cup was won again by Torpoint Athletic in 1996.

TORPOINT INSTITUTE. This was a flourishing organisation before the last war and fielded a team in its name. It won the Cornwall Junior Cup and the Plymouth & District League, division two, in the 1934-35 season. Back row: Albert Knott, Sid Hannaford. Middle row: C. Pidgen, 'Dasher' Rice, Albert Henley, Cliff Hall, Frank Bolton, Bert Parker, Charlie Partridge, Horace Grundy. Front row: Albert England, Stuart Gillard, Harold Lobb, Les Burnett, Edgar Bull.

ST JAMES' F.C. 1937-38. Back row: Dick Wagg, Norman Partridge, George Toms, Horace Evans, 'Dasher' Rice, Tom Riddell, Edwin Toms. Middle row: Harry Toms, Bert Bremeyer, Cliff Evans, Horace Jenkins, Jack Mitchell, Fred Pennington, Bill Banfield, Harry Morris. Front row: Ted Short, Ronald Kingdom, Frank Bolton, Stan Peach, George Trevorrow, Charlie Lowings, A. Evans, Ivor Toms.

Five

Transport

Two hundred years ago communications must have been very difficult for the people of Torpoint. Until the building of the Liskeard Turnpike in the 1760s travel to the west was hard, whilst the river would have made life difficult to travel to the east. The start of a reasonable ferry service in the 1830s must have made life much easier. For many years the river provided a means of transport between the villages and farms of the peninsula and, of course, as far up as Gunnislake. Goods were carried by boat to local markets and supplies from Plymouth brought back. Pleasure was provided by the rivers as we read from the reports of trips up the Lynher to Notter Bridge, and the Tavy/Tamar journeys to Calstock, Weir Head and the Bere Peninsula. After the First World War horse transport gave way to the motor engine. It wasn't until the 1950s that private cars began to make an impact.

RIVER CROSSINGS. Torpoint uses, and has used over the years, both road and water transport. The River Tamar was crossed by steam launches after the ferry ceased running at 9p.m. This is the *Link*, which, with the *Lady Beatrice* and the *Volta* ran this service until 1932 when the two-ferry service came into operation.

PLEASURE STEAMERS. Before the First World War and for a few years afterwards one of the favourite summer pastimes of the people of Torpoint was a trip to Calstock or Weir Head on the River Tamar, St Germans or Notter Bridge on the River Lynher or even on the River Yealm. Paddle steamers predominated and the first one appeared in 1820. The early ones were used as market boats bringing fruit and dairy produce down from Calstock and neighbourhood to the markets at Devonport and Plymouth.

LOCAL STEAMER COMPANY. John Parsons was once charged five shillings to travel on a waterman's boat from Devonport to Millbrook. That determined him to set up his own business, so in 1884 he started the Millbrook Steamboat Company. One of his steamers was the *Britannia*. Built by Phillips of Dartmouth she weighed sixty-four tons. Until 1914 the return fare to Weir Head was one shilling and nine pence for a round trip of forty miles.

HORSE-DRAWN WAGONETTES. These were the vehicles used for outings by road in the early years of the century. Sporting their buttonholes, these gentlemen are about to set off from the Jubilee Inn, complete with trumpeter. The first mention in a Trade Directory of Stivey's shop was in 1914, so that gives an idea of when this trip might have taken place.

MR HARRIS' BUS. The first bus service out of Torpoint ran from the town to Tregantle Fort. It was provided by the Antony Express belonging to Mr H. Harris. It was an Austin, two ton, reg. no. AF 879. It was built in 1919 and intended for Russia but was never delivered to that destination.

THE SCOUTS. Mr Harris, who lived at Claderic House in Antony, had a fleet of omnibuses called the Scouts, numbered one to four. This one, with the gleaming lamps and horn, is Scout No.1, driven by Mr Ern Goodman. After 1919, Mr Harris ran a service from Torpoint to Crafthole. His company came to a sudden end when the garage was destroyed in the early 1930s.

THE ANTONY SUNFLOWER. The driver was Mr Ted Short and Mr Granger has been identified as a gentleman sitting near the front of the vehicle. Inspector Broad is clearly checking that all is well. Let us hope that the ladies had their hats well anchored by hat pins and that the solid tyres did not give them too bumpy a ride.

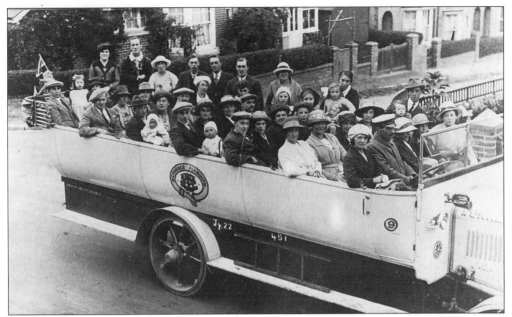

A LARGER CHARABANC. This was needed to take the Independent Order of Good Templars on one of their summer outings in the 1920s. This one was hired from Turners of Plymouth.

CHARA FOR HIRE. This is a Daimler owned by Mr Harris. It is seen at Devonshire's Garage just before the outbreak of the First World War. The driver is Mr Claude Hosking.

THE PEACH. This photograph was taken outside Molesworth Terrace, the home of Mr Hosking. He owned the *Peach* and here members of the Congregational church are ready to set off. Mr Hosking was also one of Torpoint's taxi drivers with premises in Tamar Street.

FIRST AND LAST GARAGE. Motor vehicles had to be fuelled and repaired so garages were established in Torpoint. This one, at the entrance to the town, was known as the Omega Garage.

DEVONSHIRE'S GARAGE. Arthur Devonshire bought plots No.s 8 to 11 Beatrice Terrace and erected a tin shed garage in 1913, next door to his shop. After the First World War he bought an army hut from Tregantle and part of it became the family home on the right of the photograph. Arthur himself is seen with his hand on the petrol pump. He and his son used to travel to Old Trafford Park, Manchester, to bring Model T Ford vans to Torpoint. They were sold to Messrs Granger, Harris and Gosling amongst others.

ROAD MAINTENANCE. The roads had to be maintained and this photograph, taken on what was the main road and is now the road to *H.M.S. Raleigh*, shows how it was done.

WACKER-TREGANTLE RAILWAY. The railway was built in 1890 to carry goods, guns and ammunition from the quay at Wacker, to which they had been brought by water, to the forts at Scraesdon and Tregantle. There were fifteen to twenty four-wheel trucks which had to be hauled up the track. One very steep incline went straight to Scraesdon Fort. There were two engines which never met because each worked on its own side of the incline. This one was based at the bottom.

FIRE ENGINE. The Torpoint Fire Brigade was formed at the beginning of this century. Their manual engine was a Shand Mason. It was pulled by Mr Downing's horses, Ginger and Rock. The horses were kept in what was known as Downing's Field, (and now called the Swing Park). The fire station is now the Harbour Lights Garage. This engine was used up until around 1936.

AMBULANCE, the first St John ambulance in Torpoint. It was brought to Torpoint from Bristol in the late 1920s. The gentlemen in the photograph are, from left to right: Mr Pidgen, Mr A. Worth, Mr L. Hancock, Mr Parker, Mr Worth Snr. These were the volunteer ambulance men and ambulance. At the time of this photograph the National Health Service had not been thought of.

NEW MODEL. This is a later St John ambulance photographed in the car park of Chalk's Garage, Antony Road.(Now the site of the Somerfield store).

GARAGE AND TAXI SERVICE. Mr Morgan was a motor mechanic and taxi driver who had a garage in the lower part of Fore Street. As can be seen in this photograph motor tours were advertised and a car was for hire day and night.

QUEUEING FOR THE BUS. In 1927 Devon Motor Transport Company constructed its depot in Trevol Road, Torpoint. In that year the company was acquired by the National Omnibus & Transport Co. to become, in 1929, the Western National Omnibus Company. By 1935 they had established an office at No.3 Eliot Square and ran services to Antony, Looe, Polperro and Whitsand. Judging by the attache cases, bags and cameras these would-be passengers are destined for the seaside.

Six

Traders of the Past

Many of the trades and traders of the past are still working in the town. Fore Street now has a number of estate agents and building societies where there used to be drapers, barbers, confectioners and tobacconists, wet fish shops, a dairy and even a saddler. Nowadays the supermarkets cover most of these items although it is hard to buy a saddle locally, or, come to that, freshly caught fish.

BOOTMAKER AND MAGICIAN. Charles Smith was a very well known figure in Torpoint in the first three decades of this century. He had a boot and shoemaker's shop at No.14 Fore Street from the 1890s until the Second World War. His civic role was as an urban district councillor and also chairman of the fire brigade committee. For many years he entertained the public under the name of 'Siro' Smith, as a magician and ventriloquist.

ELLISON'S NEWSAGENTS. This shop in Eliot Square was run by Mrs Louisa Ellison from around 1919 through to the 1930s. The shop was later run by Mr Ernest Blackler and then Mrs Nicholls. An approximate date for the photograph can be given as 1927 because that was when the Royal Oak Court Martial, shown on the placard, took place.

OLD TOWN DAIRY. Lewis Hancock's dairy was established in Ormonde Terrace by 1902. By the end of the 1920s he had a baker and grocer's shop in Fore Street. The dairy was subsequently owned by Mr Worth, then by Mr Worden.

MR KINGDON'S DELIVERY CART. Mr George Kingdon had a fruit and vegetable shop at No.59 Fore Street. This is the horse and cart he used to make his deliveries in around the town. The shop is now Trecaro's, still selling greengroceries.

DOWNING, THE CARRIER. In 1887 William Downing began his carrier's business with a regular service from Ferry Street to Plymouth, Stonehouse and Devonport on Mondays, Wednesdays, Fridays and Saturdays. By the turn of the century it was a daily service. His son, Harry, took over and his son, Frank, followed in his footsteps. William used horses which were stabled in Hooper Street at the rear of the King's Arms (shown here), but they spent much time in what most older people in Torpoint know as Downing's Field, correctly called Cambridge Field. In this photograph, which was probably taken around 1906, William is sitting on the shaft, son Harry holding the horse and in the cart are William Jnr, Hector, Arthur and Frank.

MOTOR AND CYCLE ENGINEER. Arthur Devonshire built and sold bicycles from his shop in Beatrice Terrace. He also sold rifles and Zonophones. He later established the garage next door. Mr Devonshire is standing by the child on the motor cycle. Note the early telephone number, Torpoint 2. Torpoint 1 was the number of the Telephone Exchange.

BAKER'S CARTS. Daily deliveries were made all round the streets of Torpoint by these baker's roundsmen, with their handcarts and baskets, from Granger's bakery.

GRANGER'S BAKERY. Arthur Granger, seen here with his wife and son, Francis, was the seventh child of Francis Granger. Francis opened his first bakery in Tamar Street in the 1860s. By 1873 he had moved to No.47 Fore Street and the family ran that shop for over eighty years. By 1890 Francis had died and his widow, Jane, took over the business, and it was run as J. Granger & Son for many years.

JOHNNO. Salvatore Marino came to this country from his native Italy at the age of fourteen. He lived in Plymouth and came to Torpoint selling ice cream. His ornate cart was a familiar sight on the corner by the Wesleyan chapel. Boys used to wait for him at the ferry in order to push his cart up to Fore Street and earn a penny ice for their trouble. He sold hot chestnuts from it in the winter. It is thought that the young men in the picture are Frank Searle and Bert Cardew. The Wayside Pulpit notice was most appropriate for Johnno: 'God's choicest plants often live in the shade'.

NEWSAGENT AND PHOTOGRAPHER. This newsagent's and general shop at No.66 Fore Street was run by Mr Joseph Worms from the mid-1920s. His son, Vivian, took over from him and is seen here outside the shop at Christmas time. Viv was well known as a photographer working up until the 1960s. He also worked with Mr Stan Hosking, who had a pilot's licence and plane, taking aerial photographs.

CORONATION, 1953. No.66 Fore Street was now run by Mrs M. Jenkins. Here she is seen standing by one of the windows decorated for the coronation of Queen Elizabeth II. This has been a newsagent's shop ever since the end of the First World War.

REDDING'S HARDWARE. Mr Joseph Redding opened his hardware shop at No.9 Fore Street before 1910. On his death, his wife and son carried on the business. His son Arthur served in the Second World War and returned to run the shop until his retirement in the 1980s. Here the shop is decorated for the coronation of King George Vl and Queen Elizabeth.

HENDER'S BUTCHERS. In the 1890s and the early years of the century Richard Hender had his butcher's shop in Fore Street. Later he moved to Harvey Street at the rear of what is now the Co-op. The authors are not sure whether this photograph is of the Fore Street or the Harvey Street premises.

NO.56 FORE STREET. For over fifty years this had been a grocer's and baker's shop run by the Gosling family. In the second half of the 1920s it was owned by Thomas Haydon as a draper's shop. Many ladies in Torpoint have memories of buying a hat for a special occasion in Haydon's. The young lady on the right has been identified as Dorothy Bennet and the one on the left as Melita Eustace. During the last war the Food Office was situated here. In latter years it has been a chemist's shop.

STILL A BAKER'S SHOP. Charles Veal opened his first confectioner's shop at No.18 Fore Street in the second half of the 1920s. By 1930 he had moved next door and taken over No.19 from Mr Jeffery. By 1935 he had opened a bakery at No.49 Fore Street. The shop was later run by his daughter and son-in-law, Mr and Mrs Hancock. Mrs Veal is seen here with two of her assistants. The shop is now Warren's bakery.

THE HANDY STORES. Mrs Mary Swain ran the Handy Stores at No.58 Fore Street (now the Ferry Stop fish and chip shop) in the late 1920s and 1930s. As the photograph shows a variety of fancy goods were sold. To the right of this window was a smaller one, stacked with books as the shop had its own lending library. The assistants pictured here are Peggy Madge and Nellie Jillard.

ELECTRICITY SHOWROOM. No.8 Fore Street has been a shop selling electrical goods since 1926, then known as the Torpoint Electrical Supply Company. Later on it became the East Cornwall Electrical Supply Co., as seen here, by which time it had acquired No.7 as well. With nationalisation it became SWEB. How nostalgic to see the display of china lampshades and cast iron and enamel cookers!

NO.25 FORE STREET. This had been a fruiterer's shop since at least 1919, run by Mr Burroughs, followed by Mr Lawton. Mrs Freda Beaver took it over around 1930. She is seen here in the doorway with her assistant, Nancy Weeks.

MRS PELLOW'S SHOP. Very little has been found out about this shop. It stood in Tamar Street, where the television shop is now situated. It was run by Mrs Pellow and obviously had large sweet jars inside stocked with goodies. It was previously the site of the Eliot Arms.

NO.6 TAMAR STREET. In the 1920s Mr John Hosking had his greengrocer's shop at No.6 Tamar Street. He obviously specialised in making wreaths but also sold poultry. Diversifying was definitely in vogue then as he also advertised a hire car.

CHANGE OF OWNER. By the 1930s No.6 Tamar Street was run by Mrs Perkins and she introduced confectionery into the business. Her granddaughter has memories of her grandmother boiling beetroot in the room at the rear of the shop ready to sell. This shop was on the ground floor of East Cornwall House, which was damaged in the Blitz. The council offices were on the first floor.

Seven

Events over the Years

In a town like Torpoint all occasions, no matter how small, become events. The authors show here a small selection of events, many of which have now passed into history, but some will be remembered by the older residents of the town and one or two may admit to feature in the photographs.

NEW SCOUT HUT. The new hut for the Sea Scouts was opened at Gravesend sometime around 1956. Canon Benskin is seen with the chairman of the council, Councillor Goad, 'Skip' Ellerby, Bryant Nickells and Syd Harris.

WHAT WAS THE EVENT? A photograph taken just after the war, or even at the end of it. The authors cannot fix a date. The fire engines still have blackout masks on their headlamps and blackout screens are propped up against the front of Clarence Place. There are several RAF and other servicemen in the photograph, but no gas masks or tin helmets are carried so it is likely that it is sometime around V.E. Day. The officer taking the salute appears to be from the RAF.

THE BAND PLAYING ON THE LAWN. Formed in the very early years of the century the town band gave open air concerts at the Lawn on summer weekends. This photograph is thought to have been taken around 1905 before the bandstand was built.

ROUND THE MAYPOLE. A gala occasion at the Lawn with the girls in long dresses and bonnets dancing round the maypole. There is a piece of writing which accompanies this photograph in the archives: 'All little liberals and supporters. Sorry we cannot see the town band playing. Come lasses and lads, but they were there. These little girls are all in step'.

N.F.B.A. Cornish District.

UNDER THE PATRONAGE OF HIS MAJESTY THE KING.

President: W. C. Bampfylde Esq.

Chairman : Torpoint U.D.C.

Treasurer :	CHAIRMAN :	Hon. District Surgeon :
LIEUT. COL. BAWDEN, J.P.	C.O. N. SHELLEY.	WILLIAM BLACKWOOD, Esq.,
Bodmin	Bodmin	D.S.O., M.B., Ch.B., Camborne.

Representative on Central Council and Charity Representative :
C.O. HOCKIN, Truro.
Honorary Secretary C.O. TOM J. SMITH, St. Austell.
Assistant Honorary Secretary— H. C. ROWSE, St. Austell.

Annual Meeting at Torpoint, July 29th, 1925.

Dear Sir,

Notice is hereby given that the ANNUAL MEETING of the Cornish District of the National Fire Brigades' Association will be held at the Urban District Council Chamber, TORPOINT, on WEDNESDAY, JULY 29th, 1925, at 1 p.m.

All Firemen in Uniform are invited to Luncheon and Tea free.

Long Service Medals and Bars will also be presented by the PRESIDENT. Chief Officers having members with Medals or Bars to be presented should communicate with the Assistant Hon. Secretary, H. C. Rowse, at once, giving name and particulars as to length of service in each case, and bring Medals and Bars with them to Torpoint.

It is hoped that all the Brigades of the County will be represented, and that the Chief Officers will bring as STRONG A CONTINGENT as possible.

All Firemen are requested to attend in "full dress" (ordinary black boots).

Visitors' Tickets—Luncheon and Tea 3 9 each.

Yours truly,

TOM J. SMITH, Hon. Sec.

All communications should be addressed to H. C. ROWSE, Assist. Hon. Sec.

AGENDA—
Read Minutes of last Meeting.
To receive resignation of Hon. Sec. and to appoint his successor.
General Business.

The programme for the annual meeting of the National Fire Brigades Association held in Torpoint in 1925.

Annual Meeting at Torpoint, on Wednesday, July 29th, 1925

PROGRAMME.

12.0	Brigades Arrive.
12.10	"Fall in" on Square by the Beach, March to Church Square, headed by the Torpoint Comrades of the War Band, and place Wreath on War Memorial.
12.30	March to Carlton Villas to be received by the Urban District Council and to be inspected.
1.0	ANNUAL MEETING in Urban District Council Chamber.
1.30	Brigades reassemble on Church Square, march to Horticultural Show Ground for Luncheon, Tea and Sports.

Firemen in Uniform Free.   Visitors 3 9 per head.

MENU.

COLD ROAST BEEF.	COLD ROAST PORK.
COLD BOILED BEEF.	COLD HAM.

HOT POTATOES, SALAD, CHEESE, BISCUITS, ETC.
ALE, CIDER, AND MINERAL WATERS.

TOASTS.

To PROPOSE.		To RESPOND.
President	His Majesty the King.	
Councillor W. H. Harris, Esq.	The National Fire Brigades Association (Cornish District)	C.O. N. Shelley. C.O. T. J. Smith.
C.O. Kenyon	The Town of Torpoint	W. C. Bampfylde, Esq. Chairman U.D.C.
C.O. J. A Venn	Torpoint Fire Brigade, and Horticultural Society.	C.O. S. J. Woodhouse. W. Coaker, Esq., Sec.

SPORTS will be held during the afternoon, including a

Tug-of-War (8 a side) for Firemen only, when a Silver Cup will

NATIONAL FIRE BRIGADES ASSOCIATION. On 29 July 1925 Torpoint played host to the annual meeting of the Cornish District of the Fire Brigades Association. What a sight it must have been to see firemen from all over the county in their magnificent brass helmets, led by the men of Torpoint on their engine pulled by Ginger and Rock. Somewhere on that engine would have been Mr Leach. Some of his children are in the foreground and others stand outside the door of Mr Billy Stimpson, the bootmaker.

Bomb damage in Coryton Terrace, April 1941.

CARNIVAL TIME AGAIN. For the third consecutive year, on 27 June 1956, the carnival was organised by the St John's Ambulance Brigade. The queen was Joan Sammels attended by Pauline Bowden and Barbara Cowan.

CAMBRIDGE FIELD. This was the venue for the start of the carnival procession in June 1955. The carnival queen was Marjorie Bickerton with attendants Joyce Smith and Jean Carter.

FLORA DANCE. In the late 1940s flora dances were held through the streets of Torpoint. Photographed here are: Austen Toms, Marion Weeks, Kay May, Kathleen May, Ruth Hyslop, Pauline Brown and June Beaver. The photograph was taken in Fore Street at the top of Lob's Hill, by the electricity shop.

DANCING IN FORE STREET. It has been suggested that this photograph was taken in 1948. That year the May Queen was Margaret Leonard and her attendants were Margaret Webb and Elaine Short.

SUNDAY, AUGUST 2nd   **FOR THREE DAYS**
(Continuous Bank Holiday Monday from 1.45 p.m.)

JOHN WAYNE, ROBERT RYAN and JANIS CARTER in
FLYING LEATHERNECKS   Ⓤ
(Technicolor)
Also Marie Windsor and Richard Denning in **DOUBLE DEAL** Ⓐ

WEDNESDAY, AUGUST 5th   **FOR TWO DAYS**
ANNA NEAGLE, MICHAEL WILDING and GOOGIE WITHERS in
DERBY DAY   Ⓤ
6.15 and 9.15
Victor Killian and Bruce Kellogg in **UNKNOWN WORLD** Ⓣ 5.00, 8.00

FRIDAY, AUGUST 7th   **FOR TWO DAYS**
RALPH RICHARDSON, ANN TODD and NIGEL PATRICK in
THE SOUND BARRIER   Ⓤ
5.55 and 8.45   Saturday at 2.55
Also **WHITE CONTINENT** and **OBERAMMERGAU** Ⓣ
Both in Technicolor.   5.00 and 7.50.   Saturday at 2.00

SUNDAY, AUGUST 9th   **FOR THREE DAYS**
TREVOR HOWARD, RICHARD ATTENBOROUGH, JOAN RICE in
GIFT HORSE   Ⓣ
6.00 and 9.10   Sunday at 4.35 and 7.45
Also Roddy McDowall in **STEEL FIST** Ⓣ 4.50, 7.55. Sun. 3.10, 6.15

WEDNESDAY, AUGUST 12th   **FOR TWO DAYS**
DANA ANDREWS, DOROTHY McGUIRE and FARLEY GRANGER in
I WANT YOU   Ⓤ
5.00 and 8.25
Also Dick Powell and Rhonda Fleming in **CRY DANGER** Ⓐ 7.00 only

---

FRIDAY, AUGUST 14th   **FOR TWO DAYS**
RAY MILLLAND, PATRICIA MORISON and AKIM TAMIROFF in
UNTAMED   Ⓤ
(Technicolor)   6.25 and 9.20   Saturday at 3.25
BETTY HUTTON, WILLIAM HOLDEN and DOROTHY LAMOUR in
THE FLEET'S IN   Ⓤ
4.50 and 7.45   Saturday at 1.50

SUNDAY, AUGUST 16th   **FOR THREE DAYS**
TONY MARTIN and JANET LEIGH in
TWO TICKETS TO BROADWAY   Ⓤ
(Technicolor)   5.00 and 8.35   Sunday at 4.35 and 8.05
ROBERT MITCHUM, ROBERT RYAN and LIZABETH SCOTT in
THE RACKET   Ⓐ
7.00 only.   Sunday at 3.05 and 6.35

PROGRAMMES for the Regal cinema in early August 1953. Torpoint's cinema, originally called the 'Peoples' Palace of Pictures and Varieties' was built by Mr Teddy Ives, a local coach proprietor and shopkeeper. It was opened in the first week of February 1920, by chairman of the council, Mr Charles Smith. It seated 550 people. As you can see it changed its programme three times a week. For many years stage shows were held on Sundays. It was later named the Regal cinema.

PEDRO THE FISHERMAN. The ladies of the Co-operative Guild were regular entrants in the town carnivals. Enjoying themselves on this float are Mesdames Hancock, Johnson, Pidgen, Pooley, Jones, Paul, Hines, Truscott, Harvey and Osborne.

BABES IN THE WOOD. The Torpoint branch of the Co-operative Guild also entertained the townsfolk with their pantomimes. Here they staged *Babes in the Wood* at the Council Hall. Among those on stage are Mesdames Ellison, Godfrey, Andrew, Fellows, Toms, Williams, Hoblin, Rogers, Ralph, Warne, Brown, Beaton and Sheriff with assistance from Sandie Curwood, Pauline Trevorrow and Carol Middleton.

CORONATION YEAR PAGEANT. A 'Pageant of Noble Womanhood' took place at St James church to celebrate the coronation year of 1953. In this scene Queen Victoria was portrayed by Mrs S. Noyce, and the young ladies with her were Marilyn Gliddon, Diane Farleigh, Priscilla Truscott, Hilary Cudlip, Felicity Truscott, Margaret Blackler and Shirley Hacker.

CORONATION YEAR PAGEANT. A further year from the pageant produced by Revd Elias Truscott. Queen Bertha, portrayed by Mrs M. Vinton, Saint Margaret by Mrs P. Cudlip and Queen Boadicea by Muriel Weeks were attended by Rosemary Blackler, Hilary Cudlip, Anita Soden and Ann Bolton. The two seated are unidentified.

V.E. STREET PARTY. Like many of the streets in Torpoint, Buller Road held its street party to celebrate the end of the Second World War. Chairman of the Urban District Council, Councillor Daniel Barr Peacock is watching his wife cut the cake. To their left are Mr Albert Ward, his daughter Emmie and her husband Reg Fuzzard. Mrs Humpherson is standing by the gate and on the right Mrs May Tope is holding Roy in her arms.

BABYLAND. For many years after the First World War and into the 1920s, baby shows were held in Torpoint. They were usually held in the vicarage grounds under the auspices of the vicar, the Revd 'Monty' May (seen here in the centre of the back row), or run by Dr Felix Jones.

HORTICULTURAL SHOW. The Antony, Torpoint and District Horticultural Society held shows before the First World War. After a break for the war years it was revived in 1919. The area involved was Antony, Torpoint, Crafthole, St John, Wilcove and Sheviock. 'Indus' Field was between what is now the Community school and 'Tanks' corner. The previous year the show had been held near Penny Cross.

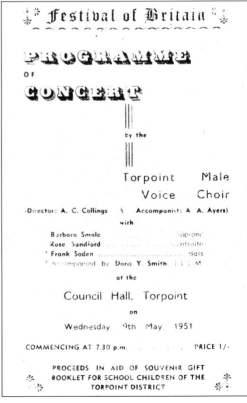

Festival of Britain

PROGRAMME

OF

CONCERT

by the

Torpoint   Male
Voice   Choir

(Director: A. C. Collings   &   Accompanist: A A. Ayers)

with

Barbara Smale .... Soprano
Rose Sandiford .... Contralto
Frank Soden .... Bass
Accompanied by Doris Y. Smith, L.L.C.M

at the

Council Hall, Torpoint

on

Wednesday   9th May, 1951

COMMENCING AT 7.30 p.m.   .   .   .   .   PRICE 1/-

PROCEEDS IN AID OF SOUVENIR GIFT
BOOKLET FOR SCHOOL CHILDREN OF THE
TORPOINT DISTRICT

THE TORPOINT MALE VOICE CHOIR. This choir was formed around 1947. Its conductor was Mr Arthur Collins and the accompanist was Mrs Ayers. They gave concerts in the Regal cinema , the Council Hall and other venues around the district. The soprano soloist at this concert, Miss Barbara Smale, who later married one of the choir basses. The choir was disbanded in the second half of the 1950s.

Eight
People of the Town

Over the years there have been many colourful and, indeed, important residents of the town. Unfortunately the authors do not have photographs or portraits of many of them. Some only gained fame after leaving their home town and others were too early to be captured by photography.

DELIVERING MAIL TO EDDYSTONE. In the 1960s Reynolds Bros. had the contract to relieve the Eddystone lighthouse. Their tug-men transferred the lighthouse keepers, delivered mail and provisions. This was in the days before helicopters took over. The gentleman at the oar on the left is Mr Bill Knott.

CAPTAIN OF THE BRIGADE. Mr Ronald Kent took over as Captain of Torpoint Fire Brigade in 1903.

EARLY FIREMEN. In the early years of the century the local fire brigade presented a fine picture. Back row: M. Dawe, M. Worth, -?-, Syd Woodhouse. Front row: -?-, -?-, G. Sleep, Capt Ronald Kent.

READY FOR ACTION. Posing for a photograph outside their fire station at the top of Fore Street the men of Torpoint Fire Brigade display their Shand Mason engine. It cost £150 and the cost of all the uniforms was £46 17s 6d, with each pair of boots supplied for £1. The cost of building the 'fire station' was £47. The gentleman in the bowler is the Chairman of the Fire Brigade Committee, Mr Charles Smith. Only the horses are missing for this photograph, they would have to be brought from Downing's Field.

EX-SERVICEMEN'S BAND. This photograph was probably taken in 1922 just before the British Legion Band, which had previously been known as the Comrades of the Great War Band, was reformed to become the Town Band. Mr Alec Anderson served as the bandmaster for both of the bands.

TORPOINT TOWN BAND, AUGUST 1949. Back row: Marine Bandsman, Roy Body, Maurice Mason, John Ladyman, Derek Tucker, Mr Henley, George Pacey, Gerald Sleep, -?-, Ormond Couch, Mr Body. Front row: Mr W. Hancock, Mr W. Benjamin, Roger Sleep, Stuart Gillard, Mr W. Couch, Frank Collins, Alec Hines.

TAKE YOUR PARTNERS. Dances in the 1930s were often accompanied by the Arcadians Orchestra. It was composed of, back row: John Vernando, Cyril Roberts, Lou Foster, Mrs Roberts. Front row: -?-, Audrey Elliott, Rose Sandford, Hayward Sandford.

CUBS IN 1924. Back row: 'Ginger' Cooper, Mr Leonard Wyborn, Jack Willcocks. Middle row: Gerald Tozer, Cliff Evans, Jack Lock, Dennis Hicks. Front row: Francis Spurrell, Arthur Harris, Jim Palmer.

BROWNIES, 1917. This is one of the earliest Brownie packs in Torpoint. Back row: Hilda Griffin, Miss Tucker. Middle row: Arminelle Hyslop, E. Stone, Winnie Rowe, Marion Worden, Kath Mudge Margery Goad, Clara Wills, Katherine Horwood. Front row: Mary Hyslop, F. Down, -?-, -?-, -?-, Hilda Worth, Muriel Humpherson.

SMILING BROWNIES, 1947. Back row: Cynthia Hannaford, Evelyn Hocking, Mary Brown, Marjorie Bickerton, Ann Chapman, Sylvia May, Lorna Mitchell, Kay May. Third row: Betty Colwill, Marlene Godfrey, Myrna Gillard, Julie Nodder, Myrtle Ralph, Tina Harris, Betty Collins, Janet Cudlip. Second row: Miss Morrison, Molly Matson, Brenda Fellows, Valerie Brooks, Pamela Leach, Jill Hassell, Sylvia Pidgen, -?-. Front row: Sheila McCarthy, Shirley Mitchell, Elizabeth Francis.

GUIDES, 1934. The Girl Guides used to meet in a hut which was situated behind Webster's Garage (now the Murco Garage). Back row: -?-, Audrey Bevan, Audrey Wilsmore, Barbara Bevan, Doris Brown, Betty Pidgen, Jean Scowen, Josephine Dancaster. Middle row: -?-, Eileen Jenkins, Eileen Waldron, Rose Selley, Mrs Benskin, Lilian Travers, Kathleen Jago, -?-, Joan Chalk, Dorothy Bennett. Front row: -?-, Doreen Richards, Hetty Bevan, Pat Waldron, Joy Ryder.

GUIDES WITH BOLITHO SHIELD. The shield on the right of the photograph is the Bolitho Shield. The competition for this shield is still held today for Guides, every third year, on a different aspect of the skills they learn. This group are in the garden of Salamanca House, the home of Mr and Mrs Hyslop, whose daughters are amongst the girls shown here. Front row: B. Welham, Kath Mitchell, Phyllis Norval, Arminelle Hyslop, Win Salvadge, Marion Watts, G. Goldsmith, Beatrice Harris. Third row: Joyce Puckey, M. Warden, M. Simmonds, -?-, G. Congdon, -?-, R. Michelmore, Ella Horwood, Beryl Searle. Second row: -?-, Kathleen Rowe, Miss G. Hunter, Nurse Jackson, Lily Hyslop, Lily Travers. Front row: Hilda Worth, Mary Canley, Winnie Rowe, Kath Horwood.

MISS FIDLER'S RANGERS. Miss Fidler, the head mistress of Torpoint Junior school, ran a troop of Ranger Guides in the early 1950s. Back row: Pam Clark, Vivienne Nodder, Elaine Mayle. Second row: Miss Fidler, Pam Friend, Gloria Gliddon, Joy Sammels, Jean Ironside, Marjorie Bickerton. Front row: Elizabeth Rogers.

THEY GAVE A HELPING HAND. These are the parents and officers who helped to run Scouting in Torpoint, photographed outside the new Scout Hut at Gravesend. Back row: Jack Hines, Ben Lines, Ted Curwood, 'Skip' Ellerby, Syd Harris, Ernest Penn, Ted Hoare, Jim Nodder, Sheila Hoskyn, Gladys Andrew, Les Andrew. Front row: Eunice Rundle, -?-, Cora Leggatt, Vera Harris, Mrs Hoare, Mrs Hallett, Edith Hines, Ruby Bawden, Edna Curwood.

TORPOINT'S Henry Cooper V.C., born in 1825, joined the Navy as a boy when he was fifteen. He had an adventurous career and always seemed to be present when something exciting was happening. During campaigns in the Crimea War, as a bo'sun, he won the Victoria Cross in June 1855. He was also awarded the Legion d'Honneur. He received his V.C. from Queen Victoria at the first investiture she held for servicemen receiving that award. This was in June 1857. Henry had married a Wilcove girl, Margery Searle, and he retired from the Navy to live in Wellington Street.

CHAIRMAN OF T.U.D.C.
Mr Harry Frost was appointed as headmaster of the Torpoint Wesleyan school when it opened in 1871. He was also superintendent of the Wesleyan Sunday school. Here he is seen in his civic role of Chairman of the Urban District Council in 1913.

CHAIRMAN AT PARADE. At a parade of firemen, amongst others, was Mr W. White who was Chairman of the Torpoint Urban District Council in 1920. He was also the owner of a draper's shop in Tamar Street.

MOTORCYCLE AND MILK CARTS. Mr Fernley Bradford, known to all Torpoint as 'Fern' is seen here in Ferry Street. In the background, outside the Kings Arms are the milk carts which his family used in their dairy business. They later had a shop in Fore Street. He was Chairman of the Torpoint Urban District Council in the coronation year of 1953.

FERRY CREW. Cyril Hannaford, Jack Willcocks and Fred Furzland were one of the crews who manned the Torpoint ferry in the 1950s.

RICHARD NODDER born in Torpoint in 1851. He became a messenger at the Western Counties Manure Factory, Carew Wharf, at the age of eleven. He rose to become the accountant and manager there. When parish councils were established he represented the Torpoint Ward on the Antony parish council and became the clerk to that body. In 1904 at the first meeting of the Torpoint Urban District Council he was elected its clerk. He lived in Wellington Street and was a founder member and trustee of the Good Templars and prominent in the Order of Rechabites.

RICHARD HENRY NODDER born in 1877, the third son of Richard Nodder. He joined the Navy on leaving school and went to New Zealand. Whilst there he left the Navy and went prospecting. At Lyttleton he joined Ernest Shackleton's expedition to the South Pole on board the *Nimrod*. They reached within a hundred miles of the Pole before they had to turn back, in 1907/8. On his return he joined the Merchant Navy as Second Officer. He offered his services to Captain Robert Scott but his health was not good enough to go on that expedition. He died of pneumonia in 1910.

WOMEN'S CO-OPERATIVE GUILD. These ladies are the founder members of the Torpoint branch of the Co-operative Guild. They were, back row: Mrs Underhay, Mrs Jewell, Mrs Tamblin, Mrs Sammels, Mrs White. Front row: Mrs Frampton, Mrs Smith, Mrs Clynick, Mrs Bradford.

LADIES OF THE COOPERATIVE GUILD. Photographed in Ferry Street in front of their banner are: Mesdames Hines, Brown, Gilbert, Truscott, Mellett, Davison, Pidgen, Sammels, Humpherson, Norval, Pidgen, Furze, Hancock, Osborne. This photograph was taken soon after the last war as the rubble of Ferry Street houses can still be seen.

JOURNALIST AND POET. Joe Griffin was a local journalist who also, at one time, ran a sweet shop at No.54 Fore Street. He wrote many topical poems about Torpoint events.

GOOD TEMPLARS. The Benefactors of Mankind Lodge was inaugurated in Torpoint around 1870. Their hall has now become the St John Ambulance Hall. Amongst the members in this photograph are: Messrs Fred Roberts, Murray Nash, James Hyslop, Richard Nodder and Mesdames Nodder and Hyslop.

FIRST AMBULANCE CLASS. In 1913 the members of the fire brigade were given a series of classes in first aid. This led to the formation of the first ambulance class in the town. It was run by Dr Felix Jones. Back row: S. Woodhouse, J. Lobb, F. Simmons, H. Worth, G. England, W. Thomas. Middle row: J. Saxton, W. Dawe, Dr Felix Jones, L. Hancock, J. Soady, H. Northmore. Front row: B. Parken, W. Leach.

ST JOHN AMBULANCE PERSONNEL. This group were present at the opening of the new hall in May 1953. Left to right: Bill Cannon, Alec Hines, Jim Farrell, Ron Grinter, Ron Mallett, Norman Beaver, John Fisher, J. Humpherson, Pauline Brown, Mrs Eddy (supt.) Pauline Farrell, June Beaver and an unidentified young man.

FREEMASONS' GOLDEN JUBILEE. The Carew Lodge of the Freemasons at Torpoint was granted its charter in September 1866. They met originally at the Mechanics Institute in Tamar Street on the third Monday in every month. The first master was Mr Frederick Brine, who lived in Salamanca House. In 1872 they left the Institute and rented the Good Templars' Lodge at £5 per year. In July 1874 a committee was formed to look into building their own premises and these were completed, on a site at the beginning of Arthur Terrace, at a cost of £363. These gentlemen were photographed at the Golden Jubilee in 1916. Back row: R. Humpherson, C. Squance, W. Crews, G. Davis, H. Luxon. Middle row: E. Greet, G. Rowe, R. Walters, P. Lewis, A. Cocks, C. Broad. Front row: R. Kent, J. Pearce, W. Jones, W. Lavis, A. Watson, J. Tresise.

COMMITTEE IN WAR TIME. A photograph taken during the Second World War, outside the 'Comrades' huts. It could have been either the Comrades' Committee or the British Legion committee as members served on both. The authors do not know which hats they were wearing at this time. Back row: Albert Ward, George Jones, Richard Sherbutt, Mr Blackler, Mr A. Drake, Mr Collins, Mr Broad, Frank Collins. Front row: Frank Goad, George Morton, Mr A. Rail, Lt.Cdr. Broom, D.B.Peacock, Lt. Cdr. Grinter, Ernest Perry, George Waldron, Charles Hayman.

Nine
Schooldays

The happiest days? Some may agree, others 'maybe'. Torpoint, from its earliest times seems to have had a thirst for education. Although a fairly poor town the number of Dame schools and private 'penny a week' establishments prior to state education shows how much emphasis townsfolk put on learning and doing as much as they could for their offspring. The standards have always been high, as can be seen by the results of the Dockyard and Forces' entrance exams. Torpoint could usually be found in the top results.

SENIOR BOYS, c. 1898. Mr Harry Frost, the headmaster of the Wesleyan school with his class of senior boys.

INFANT CLASS, *c.* 1916. Some of the girls of Macey Street infant school with their teacher, Miss Hill. Back row: Win Crocker, Mabel Walters, Evelyn Greeno, Bess Anderson, -?-, Josephine Robertson, Roma Vigus, Peggy Howers, Hetty Rice. Third row: Phyllis Tamblin, Phyllis Wragg, Phyllis Spurway, Violet Kelly, Phyllis Congdon, Myrtle Olver, Phyllis Kingdon, Miss Hill. Second row: Beatrice Nodder, Ivy Wilson, -?-, Katie Lott, Olive Chard, Beatrice Brewer, Edna Hingston, Celia Davis, Ruby Nodder. Front row: Maud Leach, Lily Jones, Kathleen Oliver, Una Snell, Kathleen Morton, Doris Jones, Elsie Williams.

TORPOINT GIRLS SCHOOL COOKERY CLASS, *c.* 1917. Back row: Irene Bancroft, Edith Sammels, Miss A. Sewart, Winnie Pearson, Vera Gould, Lena Giddy, Irene McCarthy, Winnie Cook, Irene Rice. Front row: -?-, Mabel Hancock, Gladys Pearn, Enid Harris, Dorothy Adams, Freda Trays, Miss Barberry.

STANDARD ONE AT ALBION ROAD SCHOOL, 1922. Class includes Fred Thompson, Bill Knott, Jimmy Veale, David Cockwell, Fred Gobey, Cyril Roberts, Jack Palmer, Blanche Williams, ? Longley, Ernie Pidgen, Mary Burnett, Arthur Downing, Pam Olver, Les Collins.

STANDARD TWO AT ALBION ROAD BOYS' SCHOOL, 1920s. Includes Edgar Pearson, Arthur Downing, Danny Lane, Jimmy Jenkins, Roy Hume, Albert White, Cecil Jones, Frank Johns, Bill Waldron, George Williams, Ceasar Nodder, Toby Lawrence, George Sleeman, Ernie Carter, Alan Greet, Alan Woodhouse, Eric Ferris, Jack Pidgen, Bert Ward, 'Tariff' Johnson, 'Snowball' Paddon, Norman Walters, Cyril Peach, George Rogers, George Davey, Les Burnett.

ALBION ROAD BOYS' SCHOOL. Back row: Mr Tonkin, Frank Harris, Bill Greening, David Cockwell, Jack Palmer, John Northcott, Ivor Brooking, Mr Warden. Middle row: Fred Farmer, Frank Johns, Bill Knott, Frank Smith, Phil Morgan, Bert Rowe, ? Painter. Front row: Fred Thompson, -?-, Edward Fifield, Ted Perkins, Ron Cooper, Cyril Roberts, Wilfred Lee, Fred Gobey.

ALBION ROAD GIRLS' HOCKEY TEAM, 1931-32. Back row: Peggy Madge, Barbara Ross, Edie Woodman, G. Murphy, Audrey Baldock, C. Cauley, Joan Bevan, Neta Roberts. Front row includes: J. Haimes, Edith Longley, Phyllis Selley, Emily Davis, J.Finch.

BOYS AT ALBION ROAD, mid-1930s. Back row: Pat Lane, Colin Barrett, Reg Richards, Roy Higman, Alan Bryant, Roy Reid, Francis Visick, Harry Pearce. Middle row: Ron Grinter, Bill Bishop, Victor Sharpe, Harry Jeffery, John Riley, Bob Madge, Graham Leach. Front row: Adrian Morris, Terry Madge, Ray Major, Trevor Warlow, Ronald Palmer.

ALBION ROAD FOOTBALL TEAM, 1936-37. The team include, back row: Eric Lock, Ken Furzland, Frank Harris, Ken Bridge, Stan Murphy, Stan Memory. Middle row: Mr D.B. Peacock, Ronald Kingdom, Ronald Carr, Bert Bremeyer, Mr Rowe. Front row: Bill Power, Ernie Wadge.

SCHOOL CHOIR, 1935. The girls' choir from Albion Road school won a certificate at the Truro Cathedral School Music Festival. The choir members include, front row: Miss Sewart (head), Barbara Bevan, Gladys Bratt, -?-, Dorothy Glanville, Molly Harding, Nancy Waters, Dorothy Bolton, Hilda Sparks. Middle row: -?-, Audrey Bevan, Dorothy Shepherd, -?-, Pat Waldron, Eileen Waldron, Mary Rowe, Joy Ryder, Audrey Wilsmore, Miss Gertrude Lee. Front row: Betty Shepherd, Margaret George, Nora Toms, Violet Davey, Winnie Underhay.

A NEW SPORTS MASTER, 1938-39. Back row: Bob Trout, Eric Grylls, Ron Davey, Russell Searle, Harry Balsdon, Herbert Wilsmore. Middle row: Mr D.B.Peacock, Ivor Toms, Graham Leach, Eric Hooper, Mr R. Eslick. Front row: Les Greet, Bill Dawe.

AN INFANT CLASS, 1935. Back row: John ?, -?-, Donald Correy, -?-, -?-, Peter Carter, Michael Collins, Tony Willcocks. Third row: Jean Gamble, Winnie Rowe, Heather Norsworthy, ? Hannaford, Joan Paul, Mary Correy, ? Fearon, -?-. Second row: Grace Jenkins, Joyce Hooper, Christine Bond, Christine Worth, Iris Doidge, Barbara Swiggs, Barbara Denton, Betty Hudman, Pamela Hallett. Front row: Ken Visick, -?-, Bernard Martin, John Hancock, Peter Hill, -?-.

GIRLS AT ALBION ROAD SCHOOL, c. 1938. Back row: Joan Goad, Betty Richards, Christine Rogers, Phyllis Kitteridge, Pauline Farrell, Frances Brewer, Betty King. Third row: Mavis Butterfield, Peggy Avent, Pamela Hallett, Ruth Southard, Pat Riley, Barbara Haughey, Pat Pidgen. Second row: Pauline Brown, Ruth Hyslop, Effie Ryder, Betty Elliott, Pearl Smith, Mamie Searle, Sylvia Cardew. Front row: Nancy Clark, -?-, Brenda Leach, Pat Carter, Betty Northcott, Elaine Short, Pamela Tunstall, Sybil Clark.

THE WINNING HOUSE FOR SPORT, 1938. Included in the photograph are: Gladys Hanrahan, Marie Downing, Gwen Walters, Miss Hudson, Audrey Elliott, Sylvia Simms, Honour Griffin, Phyllis Doney, Phyllis Tippett, Peggy Jenkins, Betty Northcott, Joyce Hooper, Jean Gilbey, Barbara Haughey, Pauline Farrell, Beryl Shepherd, Thelma Lakeman, Constance Bartlett, Phyllis Kitteridge, Doris Selvester, Thelma Portlock, Pat Riley, Molly Collins, Pat Freathy, Margaret Pooley, Jean Paul, Mamie Searle, Constance Morris, Barbara Clark, Marie McJannet, Audrey Hick, Barbara Squance, Nancy Beer, Sylvia Morris, Effie Ryder, Thelma Humpherson, Edna Carter, Ruth Hyslop.

POSTWAR SCHOOL FOOTBALL TEAM. Back row: Wes Harvey, George Pacey, Jimmy Osborne. Second row: Bryant Nickells, Peter Hallett, Harry Courtier, Mr R. Eslick. Front row: John Richards, Geoff Peach, Brian Cardew, Bernard Paige, Ron Devonshire.

JUNIOR SCHOOL FOOTBALL TEAM, 1948-49. Back row: John Waters, Alan Salt, Ken Dingle, Mr H. Endean, David Pearn, Brian Westlake, Alec Hardie. Front row: Clive Burchell, John Casey, Terry Pascoe, Malcolm Prout, David Davison, Brian Durke.

JUNIOR SCHOOL, WINDSOR HOUSE, 1946. Back row: Stan Martin, John Taylor, Michael Nicholson, Mary Welch, Sylvia Tamblin, Sylvia Squance, Jimmy Swiggs, Peter Brown, George Leach, Leonard Ellis, Billy Ough, John Ellis. Third row: Molly Devonshire, Jill Purse, Hazel Betts, Barbara Leach, Valerie Brooks, Christine Gregory, Brenda Fellows, Julie Nodder, Marlene Godfrey, Kay May, Pat Fairbrother, Iris Timms, Derek Pike. Second row: Geoff Turner, Adrian Durstan, Peter Harris, Alan Shipman, David Davison, Michael Pidgen, Ronald Daniel. Front row: Michael Gillard, Alec Hardie, Gordon Crocker, David Warne, David Collett, David Pearn, Andrew Waggott, -?-, -?-.

TORPOINT JUNIOR SCHOOL GROUP. Back row: David Bullock, Brian Durke, ? Pearce, Betty Ackland. Second row: John Bean, Heather Benjamin, Joy Bartley, Connie Waters, Ellen Callow, Brian Warne. Front row: Robert Evans, Bertie Nodder, -?-, Barry Strickland.

JUNIOR SCHOOL PUPILS, c. 1946. Back row: John Hortop, Heather Benjamin, Brian Westlake, -?-, Terry Pascoe, Ronald Daniel, Peter Bates, -?-, Colin Harris, Elizabeth Francis, Dorothy Davis. Second row: Robin Langford, Kathy Harris, Diane Clark, Janet Burchell, Sylvia Ellis, Gillian Mitchell, Rosemary Gillard, Anita Soden, -?-, Doreen Selvester, Pam Nodder, Josephine Macnamara, Brian Slee. Front row: Clive Strickland, Robert Evans, Keith Dunstan, Barry Strickland, Terry Snell, Roy Greeno, -?-, David Davison, Peter Tippett, Keith Conning. Front row: Roger Sleep, Jack Cottridge, -?-, Michael Leggatt, Tony Ayers, -?-, -?-.

STAFF AT TORPOINT SECONDARY SCHOOL, 1953. Mr R. Eslick, Mrs M. Ennor, Mr A. Jones, Mrs D. Blundell, Mr G. Pascoe, Miss J. Philpott, Mr F. Hall.

CHORUS GIRLS FROM 'PANTAMONIUM', 1955. Ann Strutt, Rosemary Mackenzie, Jennifer May, Eileen Bastard, Valerie Stacey, Ruby Warburton, Rosemary Gillard, Lorna Tyler, Rosemary Lovick.

INFANT CLASS AT ALBION ROAD SCHOOL, c. 1935. Front row: Bernard Stone, -?-, Marion Weeks, Mamie Searle, ? Finch, -?-, Alan Endean, John Harrison. Second row: Betty Kendall, Sylvia Morris, -?-, Pat Jenkins, Mary Leythorne, Kathleen May, Ruth Hyslop, Pauline Brown. Front row: David Hambly, Norman Searle, Ronnie Richards, George Paul, Charles Edwards, Ralph Farrell, Tom Bowden.

MR ESLICK'S CLASS at the Torpoint Secondary school in 1955. Back row: Ruby Stacey, Frances Grills, Mary Warren, Margaret Blackler, Sylvia Bradbury, Kathleen Callow, -?-, Rosemary Gillard, Violet Cook, Mr R. Eslick. Third row: Tony Lang, John Mumford, Maurice Daniel, ? Smith, Keith Dunstan, Tony Rogers, Joseph Marks, Colin Jeffery, Ray Hancock. Second row: Derek Waters, Michael Leggatt, Roger Sleep, Ivor Nicholls, Chris Hoare, Tony Ayers, -?-. Front row: Roy Davidson, Marcus Frost, Derek Carthy, Brian Williams, Colin Barrett.